Praise for *End Times and the Secret of the Mahdi*

Thought-provoking does not begin to describe this treatise. Dr. Youssef's analytical insight into the past, present, and future through the lens of the Bible and Quran brings the world around us into sharp focus.

Congressman Louie Gohmert

END TIMES
AND THE
SECRET
OF THE
MAHDI

END TIMES
AND THE
SECRET
OF THE
MAHDI

*Unlocking the Mystery of
Revelation and the Antichrist*

MICHAEL YOUSSEF

WORTHY®
PUBLISHING

Published by Worthy Books, an imprint of Worthy Publishing Group, a division of Worthy Media, Inc., One Franklin Park, 6100 Tower Circle, Suite 210, Franklin, TN 37067.

WORTHY is a registered trademark of Worthy Media, Inc.

HELPING PEOPLE EXPERIENCE THE HEART OF GOD

eBook available wherever digital books are sold.

Library of Congress Cataloging-in-Publication Data

Names: Youssef, Michael.
Title: End times and the secret of the Mahdi : unlocking the mystery of
   Revelation and the Antichrist / by Michael Youssef
Description: Franklin, TN : Worthy Publishing, 2016. | Includes
   bibliographical references.
Identifiers: LCCN 2015037825 | ISBN 9781617956621 (tradepaper)
Subjects: LCSH: Bible. Revelation--Criticism, interpretation, etc. |
   Antichrist. | Antichrist--Islam. | Mahdi.
Classification: LCC BS2825.52 .Y68 2016 | DDC 236/.9--dc23
LC record available at http://lccn.loc.gov/2015037825

For foreign and subsidiary rights, contact rights@worthypublishing.com

Published in association with The Gates Group, Louisville, KY.

ISBN: 978-1-61795-662-1
Cover Design: Smartt Guys Design
Interior Design and Typesetting: Bart Dawson

Printed in the United States of America
16 17 18 19 20 VPI 8 7 6 5 4 3 2 1

To Graeme Blaiklock
in deep gratitude to the Lord for
you and your persistence in
being God's instrument in bringing
Leading The Way to Australia

CONTENTS

INTRODUCTION

THE CAPSTONE
OF THE BIBLE

ATHEIST PHILOSOPHERS and materialist scientists tell us that human life is utterly meaningless. Physicist Stephen Hawking put it this way: "The human race is just a chemical scum on a moderate sized planet, orbiting around a very average star in the outer suburb of one among a hundred billion galaxies."[1]

The book of Revelation assures us that the atheists are wrong. God cares very much about our individual lives—and about the future of planet Earth. Though the world seems to be spinning out of control, Revelation tells us that God is moving human events toward a dramatic and triumphant conclusion.

End Times and the Secret of the Mahdi presents an exciting new approach to the book of Revelation. Most books about Revelation focus almost entirely on the future. In this book, I show how the message of Revelation impacts our lives today—and what our response should be.

As you read these pages, you will find a clear and relevant presentation of the major themes of Revelation, packed with contemporary stories and filled with many surprising insights. This is not just a guidebook to the future but an action plan for living confidently for Christ in these turbulent and uncertain times.

Instead of beginning in Revelation 1 and proceeding chapter by chapter, I have organized this book by the major themes of Revelation: the revelation of Jesus, the reign and fall of the Antichrist, the events of the Great Tribulation, the Battle of Armageddon, what the Bible *really* says about heaven, and what Jesus is saying to you and me through Revelation. This unique approach will help you to understand and appreciate the book of Revelation in a fresh way.

After reading *End Times and the Secret of the Mahdi,* you will come away with a deeper sense of awe regarding God's Word. You'll understand how the prophecies of Revelation merge seamlessly with the other prophecies of the Old and New Testaments. You'll recognize that many prophecies of Scripture have already been fulfilled with mathematical precision, and you'll know that the prophecies yet to be fulfilled are every bit as reliable.

Our Bible is a collection of sixty-six books written by more than forty authors in three different languages on three separate continents over a span of sixteen hundred years. The Bible consists of history, drama, poetry, law, and prophecy. Yet the Bible is one Book. God's Word is amazingly consistent, because our God is a consistent God.

The book of Revelation is the capstone of the entire Bible. It reveals the ultimate fulfillment of prophecies going back to the beginning of Genesis. Through the pages of Revelation, God has opened a big picture window on the future, and in this book you will discover how to apply these insights to your life today.

Now, you may be surprised at some of the amazing (and even disturbing) parallels between the end-times prophecies of the Bible and the end-times prophecies of Islam. You may be alarmed at the seeming connection between the Antichrist of Revelation and the shadowy figure of Islamic prophecy known as the Imam Mahdi.

But I don't want you to be alarmed. God gave us the book of Revelation not to frighten us but to motivate and encourage us. And that is my prayer for you as you read this book: May God fill you with hope, faith, and an eager expectation of the Lord's return. Again and again in Revelation, Jesus assures us, "I am coming soon."

Maranatha! Come, Lord!

—Michael Youssef, PhD

PART 1

THE REVELATION OF JESUS CHRIST

A Message from *Jesus* about *Jesus*

ONE

THE RELEVANT REVELATION

THE FRONT PAGE of the *New York Times* recently carried the headline: "ISIS Transforming into Functioning State That Uses Terror as Tool."[1] ISIS is the terror group known as the Islamic State of Iraq and Syria (in Arabic, *ad-Dawlah al-Islāmiyah fī 'l-ʿIrāq wa-sh-Shām*). When ISIS was formed in 2006, the world took no notice.

But by 2015, the Salafi jihadist group controlled large regions of Iraq and Syria, plus parts of Nigeria, Libya, and Southeast Asia, and ten million people lived under ISIS rule. The group proclaimed itself a global caliphate. Its motto, *Bāqiyah wa-Tatamaddad*, means "Remaining and Expanding," and it is living up to those words. The *New York Times* explains:

> The Islamic State uses terror to force obedience and frighten enemies. It has seized territory, destroyed antiquities, slaughtered minorities, forced women into sexual slavery

and turned children into killers. . . . [It] initially functioned solely as a terrorist organization, if one more coldblooded even than Al Qaeda. Then it went on to seize land.

But increasingly, as it holds that territory and builds a capacity to govern, the group is transforming into a functioning state that uses extreme violence—terror—as a tool.[2]

ISIS has become a functioning totalitarian government. It issues identification cards, makes and enforces laws, and even provides services like garbage collection. The Islamic State regime is brutal but provides stability. Many who live under ISIS control welcome the stability of oppression. One Syrian living under ISIS said, "They are implementing [Allah's] regulations. The killer is killed. The adulterer is stoned. The thief's hands are cut [off]."[3]

Reporter Tim Arango notes that many people think ISIS will collapse under the weight of its own brutality, assuming "that its evil ensures its eventual destruction." But all signs suggest that ISIS is remaining and expanding—and attracting new recruits. Arango quotes John E. McLaughlin, a former deputy director of the CIA: "These guys could win. . . . Evil isn't always defeated."[4] A few short years ago, hardly anyone in the West had heard of ISIS. Today, the ISIS reign of terror crosses national borders, enforcing its rule with beheadings and mass slaughter, posted on the Internet for the world to see.

Now consider this: It's easy to imagine the coming world leader known as the Antichrist enforcing his rule in much the same way.

I'm not saying that ISIS is the precursor to the Antichrist. But as we look at the scenes of horror and atrocity coming out of the Middle East and the mass slaughter of the November 2015 ISIS attacks in Paris, it is impossible not to compare those scenes with the Antichrist's reign of terror, as described in Daniel, Revelation, and other prophetic passages of Scripture.

Daniel tells us the Antichrist "will exalt and magnify himself above every god and will say unheard-of things against the God of gods. He will be successful until the time of wrath is completed, for what has been determined must take place. . . . There will be a time of distress such as has not happened from the beginning of nations until then" (Daniel 11:36; 12:1).

The book of Revelation tells us the Antichrist will be "given power to wage war against God's holy people and to conquer them" (Revelation 13:7). Is ISIS a foretaste of the Antichrist's future reign of terror? I can't answer that. I can only say that it's not hard to imagine the spreading horrors of our own time leading to the long-prophesied regime of the Antichrist.

Think, for a moment, of all the seemingly unsolvable problems of our time—war, terrorism, the spread of nuclear weapons, economic uncertainty, the gap between rich and poor, food shortages and famine, pollution, climate change, severe weather events, plagues, racial and ethnic conflicts, religious conflicts, and on and on. Years ago, the world looked to freedom and democracy for solutions. Today, the world consensus is moving away from freedom as the solution and toward authoritarian control, one-world government, and the concentration of power in a single authority—even a single human leader.

The Bible calls that leader the Antichrist.

UTOPIA—OR HELL ON EARTH?

The movement toward a one-world government began with a few individuals in the twentieth century. Sir John Boyd Orr, a Scottish doctor and politician, received the Nobel Peace Prize in 1949 for his research into improving global food production. He donated all the prize money to organizations working for a united world government. In his Nobel acceptance speech he said, "We are now physically, politically, and economically one world. . . . The absolute national sovereignty of nations is no longer possible. However difficult it may be to bring it about, some form of world government, with agreed international law and means of enforcing the law, is inevitable."[5]

In 1950, James Paul Warburg, chairman of the Council of Foreign Relations, told a subcommittee of the United States Senate, "We shall have world government, whether or not we like it. The question is only whether world government will be achieved by consent or by conquest."[6]

More recently, Lord Christopher Monckton, who was science adviser to British Prime Minister Margaret Thatcher, reported on the goals for the 2009 United Nations Climate Change Conference in Copenhagen:

A world government is going to be created. The word "government" actually appears as the first of three purposes of the new entity. The second purpose is the transfer of wealth from the countries of the West to third world countries. . . . And the third purpose of this new entity, this government, is enforcement. . . . [Delegates discussed]

10

setting up a global government so that they could shut down the West, shut down democracy, and bring freedom to an end worldwide.[7]

Microsoft's billionaire founder Bill Gates said he was disappointed that the Copenhagen conference failed in its goal to set up a world government. In an interview with *Süddeutsche Zeitung*, Germany's Munich-based national daily newspaper, Gates said:

> We have global problems and urgent needs. But the way we manage the world isn't super-efficient. Advantages and disadvantages are distributed unfairly. . . . We always have army divisions ready to fight a war. But what about fighting disease? How many doctors do we have? How many planes, tents, scientists? If there were such a thing as a world government, we would be better prepared [to fight disease outbreaks].[8]

Even the Catholic Church is involved in the effort to impose a global government on the world. In 2011, the Vatican cardinals issued a document calling for a "world Authority" (with a capital *A*) to impose controls on the global economy. The Vatican said:

> It is the task of today's generation to recognize and consciously to accept these new world dynamics for the achievement of a universal common good. Of course, this transformation will be made at the cost of a gradual, balanced transfer of a part of each nation's powers to a world

Authority. . . . This development . . . will not come about without anguish and suffering. . . . Only a spirit of concord that rises above divisions and conflicts will allow humanity to be authentically one family and to conceive of a new world with the creation of a world public Authority at the service of the common good.[9]

What none of these proponents of a one-world government seems to consider, much less have an answer for, is the question: How do we make sure this "world Authority" rules wisely and benevolently? These utopians make an unthinking assumption that their world government will be run by people of goodwill. But history shows that big governments tend to produce either clumsy and inefficient bureaucracies or ruthlessly oppressive dictatorships. A one-world government would be the biggest government the world has ever seen. What guarantees do these one-worlders offer that their utopian vision won't actually produce hell on earth?

In fact, if the utopians get their way, hell on earth is *exactly* what they will achieve. The result is foretold in Revelation 13: "The beast [*the Antichrist*] was given a mouth to utter proud words and blasphemies and to exercise its authority for forty-two months. . . . And it was given authority over every tribe, people, language and nation" (Revelation 13:5, 7). The oppressive reign of the Antichrist is the goal toward which the one-worlders are working—whether they know it or not.

Though current events seem to be leading us straight toward the events described in Revelation, we should avoid treating Revelation as an oracle of future events. Revelation is not a puzzle to be solved but a message to be applied to our daily lives. Though most of Revelation deals with future events, this book is not primarily about the future. It's about the present—*your* present, your life right now.

So let me make a bold statement at the outset: If your life has not been changed in a major way by the time we have finished our study of Revelation, you probably need to examine your life. If you can study Revelation without being impacted in your relationship with God, then (as the apostle Paul said) it's time to examine yourself to see if you are truly in the faith (2 Corinthians 13:5).

PAST, PRESENT, AND FUTURE

Between the bookends of Genesis and Revelation, the Bible spans the history of the human race. Genesis tells the story of humanity's creation and fall. Revelation describes the redemption and eternal destiny of all believers.

In Revelation 1:19, the Lord Jesus describes to John the vast scope of the vision He is about to reveal: "Write, therefore, what you have seen [*the past*], what is now [*the present*] and what will take place later [*the future*]." These three aspects of time—past, present, and future—are important concepts in the Bible.

The Scriptures teach that our salvation is a past, present, and future salvation. We *have been* saved, we *are being* saved, and we *shall be* saved. We *were* changed into new creations when we were saved, we *are being* changed through a process of sanctification, and we *shall be* changed at the resurrection.

The kingdom of God is past, present, and future. Two thousand years in the past, Jesus announced, "The kingdom of God has come near" (Mark 1:15). Yet the kingdom is among us right now, as God reigns in our hearts today. And the kingdom of God is coming in all its majesty in the future, when King Jesus reigns.

We learn and grow from past mistakes. We walk with God in the present. And we look forward to the fulfillment of God's promises for the future. Past, present, and future—God weaves all three dimensions of our lives into a beautiful tapestry for His glory.

In the same way, the events in Revelation have happened in the past, they are happening now, and they will happen with increasing intensity in the future. Take, for example, the Great Tribulation—a time of extreme persecution and global calamity in the future.

But the Tribulation is also a past and present event. Christians in the first century were thrown to hungry lions or crucified or dipped in tar and burned alive for the Roman emperor Nero's amusement. The believers in Thessalonica suffered such intense persecution that they feared they had missed the Lord's return— they believed they were in the Great Tribulation. Paul wrote the second chapter of 2 Thessalonians to reassure them that they had not missed the Second Coming.

And what about today? Every year, more than one hundred thousand Christians around the world are martyred for their faith.[10] More Christians have been martyred for Christ in the past hundred years than in the previous nineteen hundred years of Christian history combined.[11] And persecution is on the increase.

I have received numerous reports from people who are ministering in Iraq. One Christian worker, who cannot be named for the worker's own safety, told me about twelve-year-old Christian boys who were ordered by ISIS to recite the Shahada, the Islamic declaration of faith, or be crucified. The boys refused, saying, "No, we love Jesus!" So ISIS crucified the boys in front of their parents' eyes. For those Christian children and their parents, the Great Tribulation is going on right now.

In February 2015, ISIS kidnapped twenty-one Coptic Christian Egyptians and beheaded them by the seashore in Libya, then posted videos of the executions. The Christian martyrs shouted, "*Ya Rabbi Yasou!* (O my Lord Jesus!)" as the blades came down.[12] Two months later, ISIS beheaded thirty Ethiopian Christians in Libya.[13] As Revelation 20:4 tells us, "I saw the souls of those who had been beheaded because of their testimony about Jesus and because of the word of God." For those believers, the Great Tribulation is now.

All around the world, Christians are being slaughtered on a daily basis—and most of these atrocities are not reported on American news channels. For these Christians, the Great Tribulation is not some future prophetic event. They wake up every morning and wonder if this is the day their children will be murdered or they will be tortured for Christ.

Yet the horrors committed against Christians in the past and the present are just a foretaste of the Tribulation we read about in the book of Revelation. Jesus told John, "Write, therefore, what you have seen, what is now and what will take place later" (Revelation 1:19). The book of Revelation is relevant to the past, to the present, and to the future.

THE APOSTLE WHO RECEIVED THE VISION

The Greek word for *revelation* is *apokálypsis*, which is why the book of Revelation is also known as "The Apocalypse of St. John." The words *revelation* and *apocalypse* have the same meaning—the unveiling of something that has been hidden.[14] In a popular sense, the word *apocalypse* has come to be synonymous with the end of the world. But the word originally referred to the disclosure of a mystery. The book of Revelation is the unveiling of God's plan for the future.

Some people refer to this book as "Revelations," plural, but that is incorrect. The last book of the Bible is one Revelation, singular. It is God's revelation of the final stages of His program for human history. This book is both timely and timeless—it relates to the times in which we live and deals with universal truths that never become obsolete.

Though the prophetic events in Revelation have not yet been fulfilled, we know that everything written in this book will come to pass. God will keep His Word. How can we be sure? Because God has always kept His Word in the past. Many of the prophecies of the Old Testament have already been fulfilled. For example, the Old Testament predicted that the Messiah would:

- be born of a virgin in Bethlehem (Isaiah 7:14; Micah 5:2)
- preach the good news to the poor (Isaiah 61:1)
- restore sight to the blind (Isaiah 35:5)
- be wounded for our transgressions (Isaiah 53:5)
- be crucified on a cross (Psalm 22:16)
- be forsaken by the Father (Psalm 22:1)
- be buried (Isaiah 53:8–9)
- rise again (Psalm 16:10)

Every one of these prophecies has come to pass. Yet many Old and New Testament prophecies have not been fulfilled, because they are prophecies of the Lord's Second Coming. They will come to pass. There's no maybe about it. The fulfillment of the prophecies of Jesus' First Coming prove that the biblical prophecies about His Second Coming will also one day be fulfilled.

So who is this man John, to whom God revealed this mystery? Evangelical scholars generally agree that this is none other than John the Apostle, the author of the Gospel of John and the three magnificent epistles that bear his name. This is the disciple who leaned his head on Jesus' shoulder in the Upper Room (John 13:23). In Revelation, the apostle John was privileged to be caught up into heaven, where he came face-to-face with the glorified and exalted Lord Jesus.

Most evangelical scholars agree that John wrote the book of Revelation in about AD 96. By that time, all the other apostles had suffered a martyr's death for Christ. John was the only one of the original Twelve still alive. According to tradition, Peter and Andrew had both been crucified. Thomas was killed by spear in India. James the son of Alpheus was stoned and clubbed to death in Syria. Philip was executed in Africa. Even Paul, who was converted late and who called himself an apostle "untimely born" (1 Corinthians 15:8 ESV), was beheaded in Rome by this time.[15]

Now in his early nineties, John was a pastor in the church at Ephesus. If you have been to Ephesus in modern-day Turkey, you may have visited the site of the house where John lived. According to tradition, Mary, the mother of Jesus, also lived in the home of John, in fulfillment of the promise John made to Jesus at the foot of the cross (John 19:26–27).

You may recall that Jesus nicknamed the apostle John and his brother James "Boanerges," or "sons of thunder" (Mark 3:17). I do not doubt that when John preached to the believers in Ephesus, he thundered! In his later years, one of the spiritual dangers John thundered against was the great persecution that began when the Roman emperor Domitian ascended to the throne.

Domitian was the brother of Titus, the Roman general who destroyed Jerusalem and its temple in AD 70 (just as Jesus had prophesied in Matthew 24:2). Titus and Domitian were both sons of Emperor Vespasian. After Vespasian died, Titus became emperor, reigned for two years, then died from a mysterious illness (some historians think Domitian poisoned Titus). After Titus died, his brother Domitian became emperor.

At the beginning of his reign, Emperor Domitian demanded that everyone throughout the Roman Empire worship him as a god. The people were commanded to burn incense before statues of the emperor, and they were to chant to the statues, "Our lord and god." Domitian was a vain and ruthless tyrant who ordered mass executions as casually as most people would swat a fly. He imposed severe punishments on any who disobeyed him.[16]

But John warned his congregation in Ephesus *not* to bow to idols, *not* to burn incense to the emperor's image, and *not* to yield to government threats. He preached that Jesus alone is worthy of worship and that Jesus alone is the truth in the midst of a culture of lies.

To Emperor Domitian, the apostle was a dangerous subversive

who had to be silenced. So he exiled John to Patmos, an island in the Aegean Sea. We tend to picture John as being cast ashore on a rocky, barren desert island. In fact, the island of Patmos was a thriving Roman colony with homes, shops, temples, and an army outpost. John was free to move about the island, but he couldn't leave. As long as Domitian was emperor, John was stuck on Patmos.[17]

So John wrote the book of Revelation against the backdrop of intense persecution. The Lord gave John a message to deliver to the seven churches. That message can be summed up in two words: *don't compromise.*

When Emperor Domitian commanded that incense be burned before his image as an act of worship, many Christians said, "What harm would it do to burn a little incense? I still go to church and pray. If I defy the emperor, I might lose friends, lose business, and lose my job. If burning a little incense keeps the government off my back, what's the harm?"

But the Lord's message, delivered through John, is clear: Don't compromise. Take a stand for the truth. Stop worrying about what other people think. Stop worrying about what the government may do to you. Instead, consider what you will lose eternally if you compromise the truth.

That's still His message to us today: Don't compromise. Stand firm for the truth.

THE PURPOSE OF REVELATION

Why did Jesus reveal this vision to John? The answer is twofold—and this is not my opinion; it comes straight from God's Word.

(If anything I state in this book is purely my own opinion, I will clearly say so.)

The first reason is that Jesus wanted to send specific messages to His churches in Asia Minor. Revelation 2 and 3 contain seven letters to seven churches. Some are letters of condemnation; others are letters of commendation. Jesus calls five of the seven churches to repentance, just as many churches today need to repent. Two of the seven churches needed encouragement in the midst of persecution, just as some churches today need encouragement to persevere against obstacles and opposition. We will examine these seven letters in chapter 9.

The second reason Jesus revealed this vision to John was that He wanted to give an outline of future events—not a precise time-table, but a general synopsis of God's plan for human history, couched in symbolism and imagery. The Bible makes it clear that no one except God the Father knows the day of the Lord's return, and it is not for us to peer into the times and seasons the Father has set by His own authority (Matthew 24:36; Acts 1:7).

Jesus could return for His church at any moment, even before you finish reading this sentence—or He could return in ten thousand years. It really makes no difference whether the Lord comes for us first, or if we die and go to be with Him. A believer must always be spiritually prepared to face the Lord.

There are five crowns promised to believers in the Bible. They are found in 1 Corinthians 9:25; 2 Timothy 4:8; 1 Thessalonians 2:19; 1 Peter 5:4; and Revelation 2:10. The Greek word translated "crown" is *stephanos*, and it may refer to the crown of gold worn by kings, the crown of thorns that Jesus wore on the cross, or the laurel wreath worn by the victor in Greek athletic contests.[18] The crown symbolizes victory—indeed, it is a symbol of *spiritual* victory.

Four of the five crowns speak of the everlasting life we will experience in heaven with Jesus. But one of the five crowns is a different kind of crown. In 2 Timothy 4:8, Paul says, "Now there is in store for me the crown of righteousness, which the Lord, the righteous Judge, will award to me on that day—and not only to me, but also to all who have longed for his appearing." This is a crown of righteousness, and it is a reward for those who watch for the Lord's return.

John believed the Lord was returning soon, possibly within his lifetime. In Revelation 22:10 and 12, John recorded these words of Jesus: "Do not seal up the words of the prophecy of this scroll, because the time is near. . . . Look, I am coming soon! My reward is with me, and I will give to each person according to what they have done."

These verses are often quoted by skeptics and critics of the Bible who try to debunk biblical prophecy. They say, "Poor, deluded John! He thought Jesus was coming back soon, yet two thousand years later there's still no sign of His return!"

People fall into error when they fail to interpret scripture by scripture. All too often, we interpret Scripture by our own biases or by what our favorite Bible teacher said—instead of comparing scripture with scripture. Skeptics who think John was misguided have ignored the words of Peter:

Above all, you must understand that in the last days scoffers will come, scoffing and following their own evil desires. They will say, "Where is this 'coming' he promised? Ever since our ancestors died, everything goes on as it has since the beginning of creation." . . .

But do not forget this one thing, dear friends: With the Lord a day is like a thousand years, and a thousand years are like a day. The Lord is not slow in keeping his promise, as some understand slowness. Instead he is patient with you, not wanting anyone to perish, but everyone to come to repentance.

But the day of the Lord will come like a thief. (2 Peter 3:3–4, 8–10)

The objections of scoffers and skeptics have already been answered in God's Word. Again and again, the Lord Jesus told His followers that His return would be sudden and unexpected, and only those who were waiting for Him would be ready. We must always be ready for the Lord's return.

THE SIGNS OF THE TIMES

Though Jesus could come at any time, we must acknowledge that the signs of the times seem to be aligning for His return. It's easy to imagine current trends tipping the world into the events of the Great Tribulation.

For example, those who pay attention to the global debt crisis can easily envision the global economic collapse described in Revelation 18. In the year 2000, such a global economic calamity would not have seemed likely. At that time, the United States federal debt stood at $5.629 trillion or about 32.5 percent of gross domestic product, and the US Treasury was running surpluses, not deficits.[19]

But as I write these words in 2015, the federal debt stands at $18.2 trillion dollars or 103 percent of gross domestic product.[20] Uncontrolled entitlement spending will explode the debt sky-high within the next few years. Unless the government quickly and drastically cuts spending, the US economy will collapse and take the rest of the world down with it. That global economic meltdown may well be prophesied in Revelation 18.

And there are other trend lines leading to the events in Revelation. Every day, there is more bad news from the Middle East—the region where human history began and where it will all end. Just a few years ago, it seemed that the nation of Israel had many friends in the world, and none more reliable than the United States. Today, Israel seems all but isolated—and the United States and other nations of the world are making deals with the devil, like Judas bargaining away the life of Jesus.

From Syria to Iraq to North Africa, barbarians with a seventh-century ideology use twenty-first-century weapons to force the greatest nations on earth to submit. A spirit of delusion is spreading around the world. It's not hard to imagine how one persuasive world leader might declare himself a savior, deceiving multitudes.

Paul said in 2 Thessalonians 2:3 (KJV) that in the church there would be a "falling away" (*apostasia*) from the faith before the Day of the Lord. (This is where we get the word *apostasy*, meaning defection from the true faith.) We already see a great falling away in the evangelical church today. Many churches that once preached the pure gospel of Jesus Christ have defected. Increasingly, churches treat sin as a virtue and virtue as sin. Apostasy has infected the church.

One of Satan's most ingenious deceptions is a movement to merge Christianity and Islam into a single religious travesty called Chrislam. For several years, churches in the United States and Canada have been placing the Quran next to the Bible in the pews. Ministers have been preaching the words of Muhammad side by side with the words of Jesus. Just a few years ago, such brazen heresy would have been unthinkable. Today it's called "tolerance."

In America today, we see government officials trampling the First Amendment rights of citizens in ways that would have been unthinkable a few years ago. In November 2014, the city of Atlanta punished Kelvin Cochran, one of America's most decorated firefighters, for writing a book about the Bible's perspective on sexuality, including homosexuality. For exercising his First Amendment rights (freedom of religion, speech, and the press), Cochran was suspended for thirty days without pay. Though the city found no evidence that he discriminated against homosexual firefighters, the mayor of Atlanta fired him.[21]

Was this a violation of Cochran's constitutional rights? Absolutely. Chief Cochran was forbidden to express his religious views, even though they did not hinder him in performing his professional duties. In the future, we can expect to see the government at all levels punishing Christians for their beliefs.

Denying Christians the right to follow their conscience would have been unthinkable a few years ago. Today, religious liberty is endangered in America as the First Amendment takes a backseat to political correctness.

Current headlines are filled with evidence that society is on a collision course with the book of Revelation. I have not lost hope that these trends can be reversed. I pray night and day, for the sake of my children and grandchildren, that God will bring revival to America and reverse our downward course. But as yet, I see no sign that America is slowing its headlong rush to moral depravity and the persecution of Christians.

If these trends are not reversed, the events in the book of Revelation may come to pass sooner than we expect.

COMPLETING THE REVELATION OF CHRIST

From the looming debt crisis to the rise of militant political Islam, from apostasy within the church to oppression against the church, the world is moving toward the fulfillment of the book of Revelation. Why is all this spiritual and moral upheaval taking place at the same time? The Bible doesn't tell us, but here's my opinion:

I believe Satan is intensifying his actions against Christians because he senses that time is growing short. Satan can read the Bible as well as we can, and he knows that Revelation 20:10 predicts his doom in the lake of fire (NKJV). He is desperate to do as much damage as he can, to cause as much suffering as he can, and to take as many souls with him as he can. That, I believe, is why we are seeing increasing satanic activity in the world today.

Many churches are uncomfortable with the teachings of Revelation. These churches do not mind worshipping a helpless baby in a manger or a helpless body on a cross. Neither the baby Jesus nor the crucified Jesus makes any demands. But the risen and glorified King of kings and Lord of lords, the Righteous Judge of Revelation, demands our all.

Some in the more "progressive" quarters of the church are disturbed by the thought that this same Jesus who hung on the cross will one day sit in judgment over the human race. The books will be opened, and He will judge every human being who ever lived. There will be no excuses to hide behind. Jesus will judge righteously, and all who have not received Him as Savior and Lord will give an accounting to Him as Judge.

In 2 Corinthians 5:16, Paul writes, "So from now on we regard no one from a worldly point of view. Though we once regarded Christ in this way, we do so no longer." Paul is telling us that we must no longer regard Christ as merely the baby in the manger or the man on the cross. We regard Him as the risen and glorified Lord, the returning King.

Revelation is an indispensable book. If we did not have Revelation, we would have an incomplete picture of Jesus Christ and the Christian faith. The Old Testament presents a picture of Jesus, the promised Messiah. The Gospels present a picture of Jesus, the Teacher, the Leader, the Servant, the Crucified and Risen One. In the book of Acts, we see Jesus as the Ascended One. In the epistles of Paul, John, Peter, and James, we see Jesus as Savior and Lord. But only in the book of Revelation do we see Jesus fully glorified and magnified, King of kings, Lord of lords, and Judge of all.

Near the beginning of the Bible, in Genesis 3:15, God promises that a future offspring of Eve will crush the head of the serpent, who is Satan. The fulfillment of that promise does not take place until almost the end of the book of Revelation, when Jesus orders that Satan be cast into the lake of fire. If we did not have the book of Revelation, we would have the promise of Satan's destruction but not the fulfillment.

Can a person have a saving faith without ever reading the book of Revelation? Of course. You can be a genuine Christian and know that Jesus died on the cross, rose from the dead, and is coming again—and you can repent of your sins and commit yourself to His lordship. You would be saved without reading Revelation, but your knowledge would be incomplete.

The book of Revelation completes the gospel of salvation. It reveals the past, the present, and the future. In Revelation, we see Jesus no longer hanging on a cross but glorified, robed in white and gold, with hair as white as wool, with eyes that blaze with fire, with a voice like the sound of rushing waters. We see Jesus as the Alpha and the Omega, the Beginning and the End (Revelation 21:6). We see Jesus as the One who holds the keys of death and Hades (Revelation 1:18).

People in Old Testament times knew nothing about Jesus except what they read in the prophecies. Those prophecies mystified the rabbis in Old Testament times. Why? Because those prophecies seemed to present two incompatible portraits of the coming Messiah. Some prophecies predicted a triumphant King; others depicted a suffering and rejected Servant. How could there be *two* Messiahs?

We find the perfect example of these seemingly contradictory prophecies in the Old Testament book of Isaiah. In one passage, the prophet foretells the birth of the triumphant King:

For to us a child is born,
> to us a son is given,
> and the government will be on his shoulders.
And he will be called
> Wonderful Counselor, Mighty God,
> Everlasting Father, Prince of Peace.
Of the greatness of his government and peace
> there will be no end.
He will reign on David's throne
> and over his kingdom,
establishing and upholding it
> with justice and righteousness
> from that time on and forever. (Isaiah 9:6–7)

That's great news! But later in the same book, the same prophet describes the same Messiah in very different terms:

Surely he took up our pain
> and bore our suffering,
yet we considered him punished by God,
> stricken by him, and afflicted.
But he was pierced for our transgressions,
> he was crushed for our iniquities;
the punishment that brought us peace was on him,
> and by his wounds we are healed.
We all, like sheep, have gone astray,
> each of us has turned to our own way;

and the LORD has laid on him
    the iniquity of us all.

He was oppressed and afflicted,
    yet he did not open his mouth;
he was led like a lamb to the slaughter,
    and as a sheep before its shearers is silent,
    so he did not open his mouth. (Isaiah 53:4–7)

In one passage, the Messiah will suffer and die. In the other, the Messiah will rule in power and peace. How could these two passages in Isaiah be describing the same Messiah?

With twenty centuries of hindsight, we can understand why this is so. The "Suffering Servant" passages refer to Jesus at His first appearing, two thousand years ago. The "Prince of Peace" passages refer to the risen and glorified Lord Jesus. This is clear today, but scholars in Old Testament times didn't know this, and they debated these matters through the centuries.

The book of Revelation ends the debate. The mystery is revealed. The questions are answered. In Revelation, we see Jesus the Ruling King superimposed over Jesus the Suffering Servant— and it is clear that they are one and the same. He wears a crown of heaven and a crown of thorns. I am grateful for the book of Revelation because it unlocks a mystery that baffled generations of rabbis. This book completes the revelation of Jesus the Messiah.

So turn the page with me. The apostle John is about to introduce us to Jesus the Lord—and you will see Him in a fresh, new, compelling way. In the Gospels, we meet Jesus as a preacher and teacher, a miracle worker, the Great Physician, the friend of sinners, the Good Shepherd, and the crucified and risen Christ.

Now, meet the Jesus of Revelation, the Lord of the Beginning and the End.

TWO

LORD OF THE BEGINNING AND THE END

KING CANUTE was a Danish-born ruler during the eleventh century. His empire stretched from England to Norway. Though born a pagan, he later became a devout Christian. He built many churches in England and Denmark, and he sent missionaries to evangelize the Scandinavian lands.

Because of the king's success in battle, his people practically worshipped him. Their praise made him uncomfortable. One day, King Canute decided he'd had enough flattery, so he ordered his servants to take his throne to the seashore. His servants followed his orders and set his throne on the beach. Then Canute sat on the throne and waited for the tide to come in.

All around King Canute, his attendants and courtiers watched and waited and wondered. Had the king lost his mind? The tide rose. The waves lapped at the king's feet. Canute raised his hands and commanded the waters to depart. Still the tide rose, and the waters came up to the king's waist, then his chest, and finally his neck.

Finally, the king's attendants, fearing he would drown, waded in and pulled the king and his throne back to the shore.

Then King Canute scanned the faces of those who had rescued him. "Let all men know," he said, "how empty and worthless is the power of kings. For there is none worthy of the name, but He whom heaven, earth, and sea obey."[1]

Returning to his castle, Canute went to the crucifix on the wall and hung his own crown on the brow of the crucified Christ. The crown remained there until the king's death—a reminder of the glory that belongs to Christ alone.

The message of Revelation is that Jesus is the King of Glory, worthy of honor and praise—the Alpha and Omega, the Lord of the Beginning and the End. The Son of God was present at the moment of creation in Genesis 1:1, and He will reign over the new heaven and the new earth at the end of Revelation.

Jesus gave John this vision to remind us that glory, honor, majesty, and praise belong to Jesus Christ alone.

THE BOOK WITH A BLESSING

While exiled on Patmos, John had a vision of the Lord Jesus. When I say "vision," I don't mean that Revelation is all a dream. John had a real and personal encounter with the Lord Jesus Christ, and the things he saw and heard were not symbolic impressions from his unconscious mind. He saw reality. He witnessed real events. He truly heard the voice of the Lord.

Then John took pen and parchment and wrote down every-thing he had seen and heard, so that it would be preserved through the ages. John opens this book with a prologue, Revelation 1:1–3, and he opens his prologue with an intriguing statement: "The Revelation of Jesus Christ, which God gave Him to show His ser-vants—things which must shortly take place" (NKJV).

What does John mean by the phrase, "The Revelation of Jesus Christ"? Is John saying that the book of Revelation came *from* Jesus—or is he saying that the book of Revelation reveals *who* Jesus is? Ultimately, it means both. John received this revelation directly from Jesus, and Jesus is the focal point of the book.

Of the sixty-six books of the Old and New Testaments, Revelation is the only book that promises a blessing to those who read and study it. In fact, this blessing appears twice in Revelation, once near the beginning, and once near the end, like bookends:

Blessed is the one who reads aloud the words of this proph-ecy, and blessed are those who hear it and take to heart what is written in it, because the time is near. (1:3)

"Look, I am coming soon! Blessed is the one who keeps the words of the prophecy written in this scroll." (22:7)

In Revelation 1:4, the Lord Jesus sends a blessing of "grace and peace" to the churches. There are at least fourteen places where New Testament writers use the phrase "grace and peace" as a greeting. We find it in the epistles of Paul and Peter, and in Revelation—but we never see the order reversed. It's always "grace and peace," never "peace and grace." Why do grace and peace always appear in that order?

The order of these two words is important. No one can ever have the peace of God before receiving the grace of God. It is always grace first, then peace. Only the grace of the Lord Jesus Christ can give you peace through times of trouble and discouragement.

John goes on to describe Jesus as "the faithful witness, the firstborn from the dead, and the ruler of the kings of the earth" (Revelation 1:5). He is the faithful witness because He came from heaven to reveal God the Father, so His testimony is true. As Jesus told Philip, "Anyone who has seen me has seen the Father" (John 14:9).

And Jesus is the firstborn from the dead because He is the first to experience resurrection in His glorified body. On three occasions, Jesus miraculously raised people from the dead—the widow's son in the town of Nain (Luke 7), the daughter of Jairus (Luke 8), and the Lord's friend Lazarus (John 11). Yet not one of these people was raised in an incorruptible body like the resurrected Lord. Each of them had to pass through death again.

Jesus is the first to rise from the dead, never to die again. He is the firstborn—but not the last. All who put their trust in Him, even if they die and their bodies crumble to dust, will one day live again in a glorified body like His. We will not be disembodied spirits floating among the clouds. In fact, our resurrection bodies will be so real and perfect that the bodies we inhabit now will seem insubstantial by contrast.

The Lord Jesus is also the Ruler of the kings of the earth. Think of all the powerful rulers and tyrants who have bossed empires. Every one of them, without exception, will bow their knee to Jesus. Willingly or not, they will confess that Jesus Christ is Lord.

John goes on to say, "To him who loves us and has freed us from our sins by his blood, and has made us to be a kingdom and priests to serve his God and Father—to him be glory and power for ever and ever! Amen" (Revelation 1:5–6). Most of us have sung hymns about the blood of Jesus. As believers, we have sipped from the Communion cup—and the wine is a sobering reminder of the blood of Jesus.

But consider this: the apostle John, who wrote these words, had seen that blood with his own eyes. He had seen the blood of Jesus flowing from the nail wounds, from the thorn prints in His brow, from the gashes in His flesh from the Roman whip. When John wrote that Jesus freed us by His blood, he did not have to imagine that blood. He simply remembered it. He had seen that blood as it pooled at the foot of the cross. If John lived to be a million years old, he would never be able to erase the sight of that blood from his mind.

With that vivid image in his brain, John said, in effect, "Remember—only the blood of Jesus can save you. Only the blood of Jesus can set you free. Only the blood of Jesus can break the power of sin, shame, and addiction. If you feel alone and unloved, claim the blood of Jesus. If you feel guilty and worthless, plead the blood of Jesus. If you feel weak and powerless, hold fast to the blood of Jesus. He bled to death to give you life."

Next, John quotes two Old Testament passages. He writes in

Revelation 1:7, "Look, he is coming with the clouds," referencing Daniel 7:13. You probably picture Jesus descending from the sky amid the clouds, but that's not what this verse means. In the Bible, clouds symbolize vast numbers of people. Hebrews 12:1 tells us that we are surrounded by a "great cloud of witnesses"—a reference to the myriad Christians who have gone before us. John continues:

> and "every eye will see him,
> even those who pierced him";
> > and all peoples on earth "will mourn because of him."
> > So shall it be! Amen. (Revelation 1:7)

Here, John refers to Zechariah 12:10. When he says that everyone will look on Jesus and see Him, even those who pierced Him, John is not talking about only the Roman soldiers who hammered the nails into Jesus' hands and feet. He is talking about all those who pierced Jesus by rejecting Him, persecuting His saints, distorting His gospel, using His name as a swear word, taking down His cross from buildings, forbidding children to pray to Him in school, and so on.

In many ways, in many times in history, people have pierced Jesus. John, echoing Zechariah, says that those who pierced Him will grieve bitterly for having despised and rejected Him. They will mourn for all eternity because they blindly rejected Him as their Savior and Lord. They will mourn for having squandered precious opportunities to know Jesus. They will regret the choices they made—choices that cannot be undone.

There's nothing I wouldn't do to spare people from having to suffer that everlasting regret. Day and night, I feel a burden to tell people about the love of Jesus Christ. I pray for those who have not come to a saving relationship with Him. Once the day of salvation is over, once the door has been shut, there will be no more opportunities.

In Genesis 7:16, after Noah and his family entered the ark, God shut the door. That's an interesting detail that often goes unnoticed. Noah didn't shut the door. God shut the door and it stayed shut. Even when Noah's ungodly neighbors pounded on the door, it stayed shut. Perhaps God thought that Noah might weaken and let the people in. But God had already given Noah's neighbors 120 years to repent. When the time for repentance was over, God shut the door—and the time of judgment began.

A day is coming—a day John calls "the Lord's Day" (Revelation 1:10). When it comes, God will shut the door, all opportunities for salvation will be past, and Final Judgment will begin.

IN THE SPIRIT ON THE LORD'S DAY

In Revelation 1:8, the Lord says, "I am the Alpha and the Omega . . . who is, and who was, and who is to come, the Almighty." The Alpha-Omega statement appears at the beginning and end of Revelation. In Revelation 22:13, the Lord says, "I am the Alpha and the Omega, the First and the Last, the Beginning and the End." Jesus is saying to John—and to us—"I was here at the beginning, I am here now, and I will be here at the end. I was here at creation, and I will be here when heaven and earth are made new."

In Revelation 1:10, John writes, "On the Lord's Day I was in the Spirit." I could write an entire book on those three words: "in the Spirit." I think John tells us something immensely important in those few words.

John was exiled on Patmos because he had been a thorn in the emperor's side, teaching Christians to disobey the emperor's command. So Emperor Domitian banished John and thought he had defeated him. But John was not defeated. In his mind, he was victorious in Christ whether he was in Ephesus or in exile.

The emperor might separate John from his loved ones, but the emperor could not separate him from the love of Christ. The emperor might cut him off from Christian fellowship, but he could never separate him from the fellowship of the Holy Spirit. The emperor thought he could break John's spirit, but John was filled with the Spirit, yielded to the Spirit, led by the Spirit, and comforted by the Spirit.

That's what it means to be "in the Spirit." In spite of persecution, adversity, and loneliness, John was "in the Spirit" and receptive to the Spirit's leading during his exile on Patmos. And the Lord came to John and revealed to him the mysteries of the ages.

Here is a lesson for your life and mine: If we yield to the Spirit, no matter what our circumstances, the Lord will be present with us and will give us what we need for our time of trial. Even in exile, we can be "in the Spirit"—filled with the Spirit, led by the Spirit, and comforted by the Spirit.

John was exiled on Patmos, but his location didn't matter. Likewise, it makes no difference where you are or what your circumstances might be. You may be going through a "Patmos experience," feeling lonely and isolated, confused and weary, and you may say, "Lord, I could be serving You in Ephesus! Why am I stranded on Patmos?"

John probably felt that way too. But the book of Revelation might not exist if not for John's exile on Patmos. Often what seems like a trial is actually a blessing. Your Patmos experience might actually be a doorway to the greatest revelation of your life. Listen for the message God has for you. Ask the Spirit to make you sensitive to His still, small voice.

John yielded himself to the Holy Spirit and God transformed his punishment into praise, his pain into gain, and his stagnation into revelation. God swept John out of his own era and into eternity. John became a time traveler as God transported him to the Lord's Day.

Some people mistakenly assume that when John said he was in the Spirit "on the Lord's Day," his vision occurred on a Sunday. But the first day of the week did not become known as the Lord's Day until much later in Christian history. In John's time, Sunday was simply known as the first day of the week. So when John says he was in the Spirit on the Lord's Day, what does he mean?

In the Bible, "the Lord's Day" or "the Day of the Lord" always refers to the Day of Judgment. The Day of the Lord is that final day when Jesus returns to judge the living and the dead. We see that day referred to in the prophecies of Isaiah, Jeremiah, Micah, Obadiah, and elsewhere in the Old Testament prophecies. (We will examine these prophecies in detail in chapter 5.) It is portrayed as a time of judgment, terror, darkness, and destruction for unrepentant sinners. The Lord permitted John to see that day with his own eyes.

In John 21, the final chapter of John's gospel, there is a scene where Jesus deals gently with Peter, who is guilt-ridden after his denial of the Lord. Jesus commissions Peter to "feed my lambs" (v. 15). Then Jesus prophesies to Peter that he will one day suffer a martyr's death (vv. 18–19).

Peter clearly doesn't like the idea of dying as a martyr, so he points to John and says, "Lord, what about him?" (v. 21). In other words, "Lord, what are You going to do with John? Is he going to die a martyr's death too?"

Jesus replies, in effect, "That's none of your business, Peter." In the original Greek, this is a very sharp rebuke. Jesus says, "If I want him to remain alive until I return, what is that to you? You must follow me" (v. 22).

John records that the disciples who heard this were puzzled by the Lord's words and even spread a rumor among believers that Jesus said John would not die. "But," John records, "Jesus did not say that he [John] would not die; he only said, 'If I want him to remain alive until I return, what is that to you?'" (v. 23).

Now, this is a curious thing for John to say. You would think that if the apostle John would remain alive until the Lord's return, then it would naturally follow that he would not die—the Lord would take John up to heaven with him in the Rapture. How could John die yet remain alive until the Lord's return?

Answer: Jesus would give John a *vision* of the Lord's return! And that's exactly what Jesus did. When John was in the Spirit on the island of Patmos, Jesus gave him a vision in which he was transported to the Lord's Day, and he was allowed to see marvelous events of the future, including the Lord's return.

The Lord's reply to Peter contained a prophecy about John—and when we study the book of Revelation, we are reading the fulfillment of the Lord's special promise to John. Though John did eventually die, he lived to see the Lord's Day by being transported in a vision to the time of the Lord's return.

IN AWE OF JESUS

While he was in the Spirit, John heard behind him a voice like a trumpet. And the voice told him, "Write on a scroll what you see and send it to the seven churches: to Ephesus, Smyrna, Pergamum, Thyatira, Sardis, Philadelphia and Laodicea" (Revelation 1:11).

Then John turned around to see who spoke. He saw seven golden lampstands, each representing one of the seven churches. And among the lampstands, John said, was someone "like a son of man" (Revelation 1:13). In Daniel 7, the phrase "son of man" is a prophetically significant term referring to the Messiah.

Throughout the Gospels, Jesus refers to Himself as the Son of Man. He clearly uses that term in the same prophetic sense that Daniel used it: "The Son of Man has authority on earth to forgive sins" (Matthew 9:6). "For the Son of Man is Lord of the Sabbath" (Matthew 12:8). "The Son of Man will be three days and three nights in the heart of the earth" (Matthew 12:40). "For the Son of Man is going to come in his Father's glory with his angels" (Matthew 16:27). "For the Son of Man came to seek and to save the lost" (Luke 19:10). "Do you believe in the Son of Man?" (John 9:35).

John, who was probably the closest to Jesus of all the Twelve, looked at the risen and glorified Jesus—and his reaction is fascinating. John didn't say, "I saw my good friend Jesus," or, "I saw my Lord and Savior Jesus." He said he saw "someone like a son of man" (Revelation 1:13). Then he proceeded to describe the Lord's appearance. The Lord was

> dressed in a robe reaching down to his feet and with a golden sash around his chest. The hair on his head was white like wool, as white as snow, and his eyes were like blazing fire. His feet were like bronze glowing in a furnace, and his voice was like the sound of rushing waters. In his right hand he held seven stars, and coming out of his mouth was a sharp, double-edged sword. His face was like the sun shining in all its brilliance. (Revelation 1:13–16)

John had walked the dusty roads and grassy hills of Palestine with Jesus, but now he describes the Son of Man in terms of awe and reverence. When he sees Jesus, he sees the high priestly robe Jesus wears—symbolizing the Lord's sacrifice and intercession on behalf of all believers. But if you have never received Jesus as your Lord and Savior, for you His robe is not the robe of the High Priest, but of the Judge.

The golden belt around the Lord's chest reminds us of Ephesians 6:14, where Paul tells us to buckle the "belt of truth" around us. Jesus is not merely *speaking* truth; He is "the way and the truth and the life" (John 14:6). There can be no truth apart from Him.

John tells us that the Lord's hair is as white as wool, as pure as snow. These are symbols of righteousness and holiness. The Lord's eyes blaze like fire—a gaze that penetrates deception and sees all things.

This is, after all, the same Lord Jesus who encountered the Samaritan woman. When she claimed, "I have no husband," He told her, "You are right when you say you have no husband. The fact is, you have had five husbands, and the man you now have is not your husband" (John 4:17–18). His eyes of fire burned deep into her soul, exposed the secrets of her life, and transformed her from a fallen woman to an evangelist for the good news. She ran to her village and said, "Come, see a man who told me everything I ever did. Could this be the Messiah?" (v. 29).

John describes the feet of Jesus as glowing like molten brass, which speaks of God's judgment against sin. And the Lord's voice was like a rushing river, meaning that He spoke with power and authority. This is the same voice that called out to a decomposing corpse in a tomb, "Lazarus, come out!" (John 11:43). And the dead man rose up and walked out of the tomb. This voice spoke with the authority to forgive sins, the authority to heal the sick, the authority to cast out demons. His voice said, "Let there be light" and the universe was spoken into existence (Genesis 1:3).

Jesus holds seven stars in His right hand. What are the stars? They are the seven messengers to the seven churches (which we will examine in chapter 9). Out of the Lord's mouth comes a sharp, double-edged sword. Hebrews 4:12 tells us that the Word of God is "sharper than any double-edged sword, it penetrates even to dividing soul and spirit, joints and marrow; it judges the thoughts and the attitudes of the heart." The Word of God proceeds from the mouth of Jesus, and it pierces the human heart. That's why Satan tries to keep us from reading it.

Finally, the face of Jesus shines like the sun. John had seen the face of Jesus shine with a dazzling light before. The Gospels tell us of the Transfiguration of Jesus, which was witnessed by Peter, James, and John, in which Jesus shone with a bright inner light as He spoke to the prophets Moses and Elijah (Matthew 17:1–9).[2] The apostle Paul also saw the risen and glorified Jesus, shining like the sun, during his conversion experience on the road to Damascus (Acts 9:3–9).[3]

When John walked and talked with Jesus as one of the Twelve, he couldn't fully understand whom he was dealing with. But here, in Revelation 1, John sees Jesus glorified, magnified, transfigured— and that's how we need to see Jesus today.

When John saw the glorified Lord Jesus, he didn't embrace Him or lean his head on the Lord's shoulder as he had in the Upper Room. When John saw the glorified Jesus, he was stricken with awe and dread. He realized his own sinfulness and inadequacy in the presence of Jesus. John wrote, "When I saw him, I fell at his feet as though dead" (Revelation 1:17).

John demonstrated the awe and reverence with which we should approach Jesus. I have heard many Christians pray as if Jesus was their pal, their roommate, a guy from the neighborhood. And I've heard people abuse and misuse this word *awe*, or its adjective form, *awesome*. I've heard people say, "This pizza is awesome!" Please don't do that. Please don't trivialize the word *awesome*. When you experience true awe and reverence for Jesus, your legs turn to Jell-O and you fall on your face as though dead.

Nothing and no one is worthy of our awe but God—God the Father, God the Spirit, and God the Son. Only the glorified Lord is truly awesome. Nothing else comes close.

FOUR INDISPUTABLE TRUTHS

One day, the English mathematician, Sir Isaac Newton (1642–1727), was walking in the garden at Cambridge University when he saw an apple fall from a tree. He asked himself, "Why does an apple always fall perpendicularly to the ground? Why doesn't it go sideways or even upwards?" He realized that an unknown force seemed to attract objects toward the center of the earth. That observation led him to formulate his laws of motion and gravitation, which helped shape the scientific view of the universe for the next three centuries.

Though renowned as a physicist and mathematician, Newton considered himself, first and foremost, a student of God's Word. Some of his doctrinal views were unorthodox, but his faith was strong and his Bible knowledge was deep. In Newton's thinking, there was no tension between science and faith. In an appendix to his *Principia Mathematica*, he observed, "This most beautiful System of the Sun, Planets, and Comets could only proceed from the counsel and dominion of an intelligent and powerful being. . . . The supreme God is a Being eternal, infinite, absolutely perfect."[4]

Newton wrote several books about the Bible, including *Observations upon the Prophecies of Daniel and the Apocalypse of St. John*, published in 1733, six years after his death. In that book, Newton made a fascinating observation that all students of Bible prophecy should observe:

The folly of Interpreters has been to foretell times and things by this Prophecy, as if God designed to make them Prophets. By this rashness they have not only exposed themselves, but brought the Prophecy also into contempt. . . . [God] gave this and the Prophecies of the Old Testament, not to gratify men's curiosities by enabling them to foreknow things, but that after they were fulfilled they might be interpreted by the event, and his own Providence, not the Interpreters, be then manifested thereby to the world.[5]

Permit me to translate Newton's formal eighteenth-century writing style into twenty-first-century English:

It's foolish to try to foretell future events from Bible prophecy. God never intended for us to use His Word to make reputations for ourselves as know-it-alls. People who misuse Scripture this way not only make themselves look foolish, but they bring disgrace upon the Bible. God didn't give us the prophecies of the Old and New Testaments to gratify our curiosity or inflate our pride. He gave us these prophecies so that, *after they are fulfilled*, the glory and wisdom of God would be clearly shown to the entire world.

Newton reminds us that we need to be careful of our motivation for studying Bible prophecy. The book of Revelation (which Newton calls "the Apocalypse of St. John") gives us a profoundly important vision of present and future reality—and it gives us an exalted picture of the Lord Jesus Christ. But we must resist the temptation to try to predict when prophetic events, such as the return of Christ, will take place.

In *The World's Last Night: And Other Essays*, C. S. Lewis warns against trying to predict God's prophetic timetable:

> The doctrine of the Second Coming . . . has, in the past, led Christians into very great follies. Apparently many people find it difficult to believe in this great event without trying to guess its date, or even without accepting as a certainty the date that any quack or hysteric offers them. To write a history of all these exploded predictions would need a book, and a sad, sordid, tragi-comical book it would be.[6]

Lewis observes that the foolishness of predicting the Second Coming goes all the way back to the first century. In 2 Thessalonians 2:1–3, Paul warned about the rumors and predictions that were circulating in the church even then. Lewis also mentions the prediction of William Miller, founder of the Millerite sect, who said that the Second Coming would occur on March 21, 1843. Miller was mocked and jeered when the date passed without incident. Lewis concludes:

> We must never speak to simple, excitable people about "the Day" without emphasizing again and again the utter impossibility of prediction. . . . [The Lord's] teaching on the subject quite clearly consisted of three propositions:

(1) That he will certainly return. (2) That we cannot possibly find out when. (3) And that therefore we must always be ready for him.[7]

There are many life-changing truths that God has revealed to us in Revelation: The same Jesus who suffered, died, and rose again will come back to earth as the King of all nations. The same Messiah who was rejected and crucified will judge the world. The same Jesus who had no place to lay His head is the One who said, "Heaven is my throne, and the earth is my footstool" (Isaiah 66:1). The same Jesus who now offers salvation to all will one day shut the door—and the time of God's favor will come to a close.

Will the Lord take His church out of the world before the Great Tribulation begins? Or will the church go through three and a half years of the Great Tribulation? Or will the church have to go through the entire seven years of Tribulation? God knows the answer to these questions, and whatever His answer may be, He will give us grace to sustain us.

If God gave me a vote in the matter (which He has not), my vote would be, "Come quickly, Lord Jesus! In fact, come early!" You see, I'm as big a coward as anybody. Not only do I *not* want to go through seven years or three and a half years of the Great Tribulation—I don't want to go through one minute of it!

But the question of when the Rapture takes place is a minor matter, compared with the major themes of Revelation. Let's not get sidetracked by minor details, because then we might miss the big picture. What are the "big picture" themes of the book of Revelation that most Bible teachers would agree on?

First, all who welcome Jesus Christ as their Lord and Savior will be welcomed into heaven when He returns.

Second, Jesus will return as He promised.

Third, Jesus will sit in righteous judgment over all who have refused to accept Him as Lord and Savior during their earthly lives.

Fourth, when Jesus appears, all those who love Him will be with Him forever.

These are four indisputable truths that shout loudly and clearly from the book of Revelation. Christians of goodwill may debate the details of this prophecy, but those four principles are beyond debate.

The book of Revelation confronts each of us with a deeply personal question: If Jesus were to return today, would you be thrilled—or afraid? Do not rest until you can answer confidently, "I can't wait to see the Lord face-to-face!" You can know you are saved eternally. I want you to have that assurance every day of your Christian life.

Are you ready for the Lord's return? Do you live every day for Him? Do you share the good news of Jesus Christ with the people around you? Do you confess and repent of your sins on a daily basis? Do you ask for the filling of the Holy Spirit every day? Do you pray, study His Word, and seek to become more Christlike with each new day? Do you look forward to the Lord's return at any moment? Jesus said:

Therefore keep watch, because you do not know on what day your Lord will come. But understand this: If the owner of the house had known at what time of night the thief was coming, he would have kept watch and would not have let his house be broken into. So you also must be ready, because the Son of Man will come at an hour when you do not expect him. (Matthew 24:42–44)

If we study the book of Revelation, it will not merely increase our knowledge. *It will change our lives.* Because of the life-changing truths of the book of Revelation, you and I can live each day with eternity in our hearts.

IS YOUR HAIR COMBED?

In the opening chapter of Revelation, John presents an image of Jesus that crystallizes all that has been written about Jesus the Messiah in the Old and New Testaments. Through John's eyes, we see the resurrected, glorified, and exalted Lord Jesus—the eternal God, the Alpha and Omega, the Almighty, the Creator, the Eternal Word.

And as we continue through Revelation, we discover more and more facets of our wonderful Savior. In Revelation 5–7 and 12, we see Him as the Lamb of God, the Messiah of Old Testament prophecy, and the focus of our worship. In Revelation 14, we see Him as the Righteous Judge. And in Revelation 19, we see Him as our Commander, the King of kings and Lord of lords, victorious over Satan, sin, and death.

The better we get to know Jesus, the more eager we'll be to see Him face-to-face. I don't know when He will return, but I often wake up thinking, *Today might be the day!* The thought of His return excites and comforts me. As John once wrote, "We know that when Christ appears, we shall be like him, for we shall see him as he is. All who have this hope in him purify themselves, just as he is pure" (1 John 3:2–3).

One of my favorite theologians is a five-year-old girl I recently heard about. I don't know her name, but I admire her love for Jesus. She went to Sunday school one day, and her teacher told her that Jesus would be coming back. So she went home and asked, "Mommy, is it true that Jesus is coming back?"

Her mother said, "Yes, honey, it's true."

"Do you believe that?"

"Yes, honey, I really do."

"Could He come back this week?"

"Yes, He could come this week."

"Could He come today?"

"Yes, He could come today."

"Could He come at this very moment?"

"Yes, honey. He certainly could."

"Mommy . . . Would you help me comb my hair?"

This little girl understands the core truth of Revelation better than most adults. She wants to be ready to meet the Lord. When He returns, she wants to be sure her hair is combed. That's practical theology.

Is your hair combed—spiritually speaking? Are you ready for His appearing? That's the urgent question confronting us on every page of the book of Revelation.

PART 2

KNOW YOUR ENEMY

The Antichrist Is Not Who You Think He Is

THREE

THE ARRIVAL OF THE ANTICHRIST

IN HIS YOUTH, Ignatius was a student and traveling companion of the apostle John. Ignatius was appointed bishop of Antioch by the apostle Peter. He led the church in Antioch, Syria, for many years before being arrested by the Roman government.

There is no record of the charges against him, so the reason for his arrest is a mystery. We only know that he was led in chains from Antioch to Rome, where he stood trial. He wrote a number of letters during his journey, and though he suffered harsh treatment from his captors, God gave him the grace to refer to his chains as "my spiritual pearls."[1] After his trial and conviction, Ignatius suffered many horrible tortures from the Romans. Finally, in AD 107, they led him to the Colosseum and threw him to the wild beasts.

In his letter to the Ephesians, shortly before his death, Ignatius wrote, "The Last Days are here. . . . Let our lot be genuine life in Jesus Christ. Do not let anything catch your eye besides Him."[2]

That's good advice: Keep your eyes on Jesus. Don't be distracted by lesser things. Always be ready for the Lord's return.

But Ignatius was mistaken in thinking he lived in the Last Days.

The explorer Christopher Columbus was a student of Bible prophecy. He was heavily influenced by the twelfth-century Calabrian abbot Joachim of Fiore. Columbus became obsessed with a prediction supposedly made by Joachim that a "Last World Emperor" would arise in Spain and would lead a war to retake Jerusalem and the Holy Land from the Muslims. Columbus believed the world would end in 1656.

When Columbus set sail in 1492, he wanted to open a trade route to India—and he wanted to convert the people of India to Christianity. He believed that gold from those lands would finance a new Crusade to recapture Jerusalem and hasten the Lord's return.[3] His true motive when he set sail was to fulfill Bible prophecy. In 1500, he wrote in a letter, "God made me the messenger of the new heaven and the new earth of which he spoke through St. John in the Apocalypse [the Book of Revelation]."[4]

Columbus never reached India. He didn't know that North and South America blocked his path. He was also wrong about the world ending in 1656.

Jesus warned us not to set dates and times for the fulfillment of prophecy. "But about that day or hour no one knows, not even the angels in heaven, nor the Son, but only the Father" (Matthew 24:36). We must be vigilant and ready to meet Him at any time—and we should never presume to know the things that God has chosen to conceal.

The Lord also told us to watch for the signs that the end is drawing near. "Watch out that no one deceives you," He said. "For many will come in my name, claiming, 'I am the Messiah,' and will deceive many" (Matthew 24:4–5). He said there would be wars and rumors of wars, famines and earthquakes, persecution, apostasy, false teachers, and an increase of sins and wickedness—but these events, Jesus said, are not the actual signs of the Last Days. They are just the "birth pains" (v. 8). The unmistakable sign that the End is near, Jesus said, is this:

> So when you see standing in the holy place "the abomination that causes desolation," spoken of through the prophet Daniel—let the reader understand—then let those who are in Judea flee to the mountains. . . . For then there will be great distress, unequaled from the beginning of the world until now—and never to be equaled again. (Matthew 24:15–16, 21)

What is "the abomination that causes desolation"? Both Jesus and the prophet Daniel warned about it. In Revelation 13:15, we see that an image of the Antichrist appears to come to life. Everyone in the world is required to worship the image—and all who refuse are killed. This image is almost certainly the "abomination" Jesus and Daniel warned us of. When the "abomination" is set up in the temple in Jerusalem, the Last Days will begin.

THE WOMAN AND THE DRAGON

Evangelical scholars agree that the arrival of the Antichrist coincides with the beginning of the Great Tribulation. The book of Revelation, however, does not present these events in a step-by-step, chronological order. The cataclysms of the Great Tribulation are presented as a series of themes rather than a sequence of events:

Revelation 6:1 to 8:5 records the opening of the seven seals, which represents a time of global suffering, death, and destruction. There is no mention of the Antichrist in connection with these seals, but the opening of the first six seals unleashes a series of disasters upon the earth—famine, war, economic calamity, persecution, and signs in the heavens. As we will see, most of these disasters are the direct result of the Antichrist's global dictatorship.

The opening of the seals triggers the Great Tribulation. Just before the opening of the seventh seal, there is silence in heaven for about half an hour. In the seventh seal, seven angels take up seven trumpets, and an eighth angel takes fire from the heavenly altar and casts the fire to earth, producing lightning, thunder, and an earthquake.

In Revelation 8:6 through Revelation 11, John zooms in on the seven trumpets of judgment. We see scene after scene of devastation. When the first trumpet sounds, hail and fire, mingled with blood, burn up a third of the earth's vegetation. The second trumpet sounds, and an object like a fiery mountain falls into the ocean, killing a third of the sea creatures and destroying a third of the ships at sea. At the third trumpet, a star called Wormwood falls from the heavens and poisons a third of the rivers and springs.

Next, the heavens are shaken. The fourth trumpet spreads darkness over a third of the sun, the moon, and the stars. At the fifth trumpet, a star falls from the sky, and the bottomless pit opens up, disgorging smoke, fire, and flying creatures like locusts with humanlike faces, lions' teeth, and breastplates of iron—possibly a description of machines of war. At the sixth trumpet, an army of two hundred million rises up to kill a third of the human race with fire and brimstone. At the seventh trumpet, the temple of God opens in heaven, and the ark of God's covenant becomes visible amid flashes of lightning and a great earthquake.

Then, in Revelation 12, we meet the woman "clothed with the sun, with the moon under her feet and a crown of twelve stars on her head" (v. 1). She is in labor with a male child. A fiery red, seven-headed Dragon sweeps a third of the stars from the sky with his tail and awaits the birth of the woman's child. The woman gives birth, the child is taken up to God's throne, and the woman hides in the wilderness for three and a half years. When the Dragon is unable to attack the woman, he takes out his rage against her children, who remain faithful to the Lord.

We find clues to the meaning of these symbols in Genesis 37:9–11. There, Joseph, the son of Jacob, has a dream in which the sun, moon, and eleven stars bow to him. When Joseph tells his dream to his family, they have no trouble interpreting it. Jacob rebukes Joseph and says, "What is this dream you had? Will your mother and I and your brothers actually come and bow down to the ground before you?" (v. 10). The sun represents Jacob, the father of the nation of Israel. The moon represents his wife Rachel. The stars represent Joseph's eleven brothers—and hence, the other eleven tribes of Israel. The sun, moon, and stars bowed to Joseph because he was a symbolic type of Christ.

So the woman who gives birth to a child in Revelation 12 is Israel. The child is Jesus the Messiah. The twelve stars on the woman's head represent the twelve tribes of Israel. The apostle Paul, in Galatians 6:16, refers to the church of Jesus Christ as "the Israel of God." In other words, the church is the new Israel, consisting of believers from every tribe and nation. So the church hides in the wilderness for three and a half years, while the Dragon—Satan—rages against her and against her children.

Next, John describes the Dragon, who symbolizes Satan: "Then another sign appeared in heaven: an enormous red dragon with seven heads and ten horns and seven crowns on its heads" (Revelation 12:3).

What do the seven heads and ten horns symbolize? The seven heads speak of the impossibility of killing the Dragon. Satan is immortal—and that's why he and his followers will spend eternity in the torment of hell. The horns symbolize the Dragon's super-human powers. As the apostle Paul told us, "Our struggle is not against flesh and blood, but against the rulers, against the authorities, against the powers of this dark world and against the spiritual forces of evil in the heavenly realms" (Ephesians 6:12). Satan is an immensely powerful spiritual being.

There's an interesting aside in this passage—what might be called a flashback. John's vision of the future suddenly flashes back in time to the distant past, when Satan and his angels rebelled against God. John writes:

Then war broke out in heaven. Michael and his angels fought against the dragon, and the dragon and his angels fought back. But he was not strong enough, and they lost their place in heaven. The great dragon was hurled down—that ancient serpent called the devil, or Satan, who leads the whole world astray. He was hurled to the earth, and his angels with him. (Revelation 12:7–9)

This is the same event the prophet Isaiah described when he wrote:

How you have fallen from heaven,
    morning star, son of the dawn!
You have been cast down to the earth,
    you who once laid low the nations!
You said in your heart,
    "I will ascend to the heavens;
I will raise my throne
    above the stars of God." (Isaiah 14:12–13)

Many people are confused by this passage. They ask, "Why did John insert a narrative about the distant past into a prophecy about the future?" This is a common feature of prophetic writing. We often find the past, present, and future side by side in the same passage. We saw earlier that Isaiah included messianic prophecies of the Lord's suffering and death alongside messianic prophecies of his future reign as King of kings.

Satan rebelled against God and attempted to overthrow God. In his rebellion and fall, Satan took one-third of the angelic beings with him (Revelation 12:4). Satan and his angels were thrown out of heaven. These fallen angels are the spirit-beings we know as demons. They are Satan's foot soldiers, and Satan employs these demons to spread havoc in the world.

Remember: Satan knows the Bible better than you and I do. When Jesus was born, Satan knew all the prophecies of the coming of the Messiah. So he inspired King Herod to commit infanticide, hoping to kill the Messiah. Herod did as Satan suggested, ordering that all baby boys two years old and younger be slain (Matthew 2:16). Satan caused great sorrow and suffering, yet he failed to kill the baby Jesus.

Satan waited for his opportunity to tempt Jesus in the wilderness, and he used Scripture in his attempt to turn Jesus away from His messianic mission—but Jesus was victorious over Satan. Throughout the Lord's earthly ministry, Satan repeatedly inspired the priests and Pharisees to plot against Him, but to no avail.

Finally, Satan inspired Judas to betray Jesus. The priests arrested Jesus, tried Him, condemned Him to death, and maneuvered the Romans into nailing Him to the cross. Satan rejoiced to see that he had finally won. He had thwarted God's plan. He had killed the long-awaited Messiah.

Satan's gloating on Friday turned to shock and awe on Sunday morning. All of Satan's strategies had played into the hands of Almighty God. The crucifixion of Jesus paid the price for the sins of the human race. The resurrection of Jesus made it possible for us to have eternal life. The empty tomb was God's secret weapon against Satan.

THE ANTICHRIST REVEALED

In Revelation 13, we meet the Beast—also known as the Antichrist. The Antichrist has been a subject of many popular books and films, from *The Omen* and *Rosemary's Baby* to the Left Behind series. All of these popular depictions of the Antichrist fall short of the prophetic reality we find in both the Old and New Testaments.

It might surprise you that the first place in Scripture the Antichrist is mentioned is not in Revelation, but in Daniel. The prophet Daniel does not use the words "Beast" or "Antichrist" in his prophecy. In fact, he does not use a name for this individual— Daniel simply uses the pronouns "he" or "him." But there is no question that Daniel is speaking of the Antichrist. He writes:

He will confirm a covenant with many for one "seven." In the middle of the "seven" he will put an end to sacrifice and offering. And at the temple he will set up an abomination that causes desolation, until the end that is decreed is poured out on him. (Daniel 9:27)

The "seven" refers to the seven-year period of the Great Tribulation. Daniel's description of the Tribulation is completely consistent with the description in Revelation. Daniel set down his prophecy in the sixth century BC, yet God inspired him to write about events that still await fulfillment in our own future.

The man Daniel speaks of is the same individual John calls "the Beast" and the same person Jesus speaks about in Matthew 24. Daniel tells us that the Antichrist will make a formal covenant with Israel, and the term of that covenant will be seven years. The Antichrist will permit Israel to restore the temple that was destroyed by the Romans in AD 70. The covenant will allow Israel to revive the old traditions of Judaism, including animal sacrifices.

But halfway through that seven-year period, the Antichrist will display his treachery and abrogate the covenant, calling an immediate halt to the Jewish religious practices. At the altar where the Jewish priests make sacrifices to the Lord, the Antichrist will set up "an abomination that causes desolation" and defile the temple. The apostle Paul talks about this event, referring to the Antichrist as "the man of lawlessness":

> Don't let anyone deceive you in any way, for that day will not come until the rebellion occurs and the man of lawlessness is revealed, the man doomed to destruction. He will oppose and will exalt himself over everything that is called God or is worshiped, so that he sets himself up in God's temple, proclaiming himself to be God. . . .
>
> For the secret power of lawlessness is already at work; but the one who now holds it back will continue to do so till he is taken out of the way. And then the lawless one will be revealed, whom the Lord Jesus will overthrow with the breath of his mouth and destroy by the splendor of his coming. The coming of the lawless one will be in

accordance with how Satan works. He will use all sorts of displays of power through signs and wonders that serve the lie. (2 Thessalonians 2:3–4, 7–9)

Revelation tells us that the seven-year period of the Antichrist's reign begins with the opening of the first four seals (Revelation 6:1–8). Those first four seals unleash war, global economic collapse, hunger, and widespread death. It will be a global catastrophe, and the entire human race will be caught up in it.

The first four seals are represented by four riders on horseback. The first rider is on a white horse, symbolizing the false promise of peace. The Antichrist will pose as a champion of peace, a master diplomat, and a broker of peace treaties. For his efforts as a peacemaker, he may win the Nobel Peace Prize. He will be Satan's counterfeit of Jesus, the true Prince of Peace. The apostle Paul wrote, "The day of the Lord will come like a thief in the night. While people are saying, 'Peace and safety,' destruction will come on them suddenly" (1 Thessalonians 5:2–3).

The second rider comes astride a fiery red horse, and he unleashes war like the world has never seen before.

The third rider is on a black horse, and he brings economic collapse, joblessness, scarcity, skyrocketing inflation, famine, riots, and panic. As we read in Lamentations, "Those killed by the sword are better off than those who die of famine; racked with hunger, they waste away for lack of food from the field" (4:9).

The fourth rider is on a pale horse, the color of a corpse. As we would expect, war and economic collapse bring death.

But don't lose hope. None of these things—not even the threat of nuclear war—can separate us from God's love and His plan for our lives. As Paul reminds us:

Who shall separate us from the love of Christ? Shall trouble or hardship or persecution or famine or nakedness or danger or sword? As it is written:

"For your sake we face death all day long;
we are considered as sheep to be slaughtered."

No, in all these things we are more than conquerors through him who loved us. For I am convinced that neither death nor life, neither angels nor demons, neither the present nor the future, nor any powers, neither height nor depth, nor anything else in all creation, will be able to separate us from the love of God that is in Christ Jesus our Lord. (Romans 8:35–39)

No matter how the ground may shake beneath your feet, no matter how the world may crumble and fall all around us, God holds us securely in His strong hands. And He will not let go.

THE SATANIC FAMILY RESEMBLANCE

Next, notice the strong family resemblance between Satan and the Antichrist. The Antichrist is Satan's most impressive and frightening creation. John calls him "the Beast" and describes him in symbolic terms:

The dragon stood on the shore of the sea. And I saw a beast coming out of the sea. It had ten horns and seven heads, with ten crowns on its horns, and on each head a blasphemous name. (Revelation 13:1)

Does this description of the Beast seem familiar? Notice how it resonates with the description of the Dragon in Revelation 12:

Then another sign appeared in heaven: an enormous red dragon with seven heads and ten horns and seven crowns on its heads. (v. 3)

Both the Dragon and the Beast are described as having seven heads and ten horns. Clearly, the Dragon has fashioned the Beast in his own image. The Beast has his father's distinctive traits, but he will not be an immortal being like the Dragon. He will *seem* to be immortal and all-powerful—and that appearance of supernatural power will deceive the world and cause millions to worship him. John continues:

The beast I saw resembled a leopard, but had feet like those of a bear and a mouth like that of a lion. The dragon gave the beast his power and his throne and great authority. One of the heads of the beast seemed to have had a fatal wound, but the fatal wound had been healed. The whole world was filled with wonder and followed the beast. (Revelation 13:2–3)

The Antichrist's power and authority will come straight from Satan himself. And Satan will even perform a false miracle. The Beast will suffer a seemingly fatal wound, but the wound will be healed, and the Antichrist will be restored to life. It will be Satan's ultimate counterfeit—the "resurrection" of the Antichrist. The whole world will witness this apparent miracle, and people around the world will worship the false messiah.

Satan will pour all his deceptive power into the Antichrist, and this great human leader will become the most charming and persuasive human being on earth. Even Christians may be deceived at first. The Antichrist will be so persuasive that he will convince the masses to worship the Dragon—Satan himself. John writes:

> People worshiped the dragon because he had given authority to the beast, and they also worshiped the beast and asked, "Who is like the beast? Who can wage war against it?" (Revelation 13:4)

Both Daniel and the Lord Jesus speak of the Antichrist as setting up an abomination in the temple in Jerusalem. The Antichrist will be a paragon of peace for a time—then he will turn on Israel, demand to be worshipped instead of God, and impose a reign of violence and fear that will make ISIS seem tame by comparison.

Just as Jesus is the full expression of God the Father in human form, the Antichrist will be the full expression of Satan in human form. The contrast between the Lord Jesus and the Antichrist is instructive: Jesus is the Holy One of God; the Antichrist is the lawless one of Satan. Jesus is the Son of God; the Antichrist is the son of perdition. Jesus is the man of sorrows; the Antichrist is the man of sin. Jesus came in the name of the Father; the Antichrist came to magnify his own name. Jesus came as a servant; the Antichrist will come to be worshipped. The world rejected Jesus; the world will worship the Antichrist.

Revelation 13:2 describes the Antichrist this way: "The beast I saw resembled a leopard, but had feet like those of a bear and a mouth like that of a lion." The symbolic imagery of the Bible is intended to convey an important truth. God does not waste His words. The claws of a bear, the teeth of a lion, and the power of a leopard portray the brutality, savagery, and ruthlessness of the Antichrist.

Satan will give his power, throne, and authority to the Antichrist. The Antichrist will perform counterfeit miracles and will openly blaspheme God. He will make war against God's people. All those whose names are not written in the book of life will worship the Beast.

So we need to examine ourselves and make sure that our names are written in that book. If there is any question in your mind, I encourage you to put a bookmark right here and finish this chapter later. Turn to chapter 10. Don't hesitate; don't procrastinate. Don't risk your eternal destiny for even a second.

Settle the matter of your salvation now, then come back and finish reading this chapter.

MAKE WAY FOR THE ANTICHRIST

John makes a statement in Revelation 13 that many students of the Bible find puzzling. He writes:

Whoever has ears, let them hear.

> "If anyone is to go into captivity,
> into captivity they will go.
> If anyone is to be killed with the sword,
> with the sword they will be killed."

This calls for patient endurance and faithfulness on the part of God's people. (vv. 9–10)

To me, these words are some of the most precious jewels God has tucked into His Word. God is saying, "Believers in that day will face persecution with faithfulness and courage. They will say, 'I am not afraid of captivity. I am not afraid of the sword. The Antichrist may kill my body, but he can never separate me from the love of God.'" They will follow the example of Jesus, who told Pontius Pilate, "You would have no power over me if it were not given to you from above" (John 19:11).

You may not believe you could face persecution and death for the sake of Jesus Christ. But if you live each day filled with the Holy Spirit, feeding your soul on His Word, living in prayerful communion with Christ, then the Spirit of God will be with you when you need Him. He will give you the courage and the words to speak.

For centuries, Satan has been preparing the world for the coming of the Antichrist. He is persuading masses of people—including many Christians—that all religions ought to cooperate with one another. I sometimes hear people in the church say, "Why can't all religions unite and work together for the same goals? All religions worship the same God, and all religions are equal in God's eyes."

That sentiment sounds reasonable according to worldly wisdom, but it does not come from God's Word. It comes from Satan. I once sat in a church and heard a minister declare from the pulpit, "The one whom Christians will know as Christ is known to the Jews as the Messiah, to the Buddhists as the fifth Buddha, to the Muslims as Imam Mahdi, and to the Hindus as Krishna. All these names speak of the same person. All of these religions lead to the same destination." Then he recommended that people visit the website of the New Age guru Deepak Chopra.

Let me be clear: Our Lord Jesus Christ, who died on the cross and rose again on the third day, is not the fifth Buddha. He is not the Imam Mahdi. He is not the immoral god of love Krishna. Our Lord Jesus Christ is the pure, sinless Son of God, and when He returns, the world will mourn for having rejected Him. The teaching that all faiths are equal, that the fifth Buddha and the Mahdi and Krishna are no different from Jesus Christ, is satanically designed to deceive the world and prepare the way for the Antichrist.

The Antichrist will preach a message of peace and tolerance and coexistence. Our culture is already being conditioned to accept the Antichrist's message. Take, for example, the "Coexist" bumper sticker that we see all around. The *C* forms the Islamic crescent. The *O* is the symbol of the secular peace movement. The *E* combines the male and female symbols as an expression of equality. The *X* is represented by the Jewish Star of David. The letter *I* is dotted by the pentacle of witchcraft or pagan religions. The *S* is the yin and yang symbol of Taoism. And the *T* is for the cross of Christ.

People say, "What could be more wonderful than that we all coexist, in spite of our differences? If we could only be less judgmental and more tolerant of each other's beliefs, we would have a utopia, a paradise on earth!"

Please understand, when we practice the pure, loving gospel that Jesus died to bring us, we Christians are authentically the most loving and tolerant people on the planet. Jesus taught us to hate the sin and love the sinner. In fact, we hate the sin *because* we love the sinner. Sin destroys lives; Jesus saves.

We can preach against drug abuse while loving the addict. We can preach against divorce while loving divorced people and their children. We can preach against sexual sin, both heterosexual and homosexual, precisely because we have such a deep compassion for those who are trapped in sin. We can preach against abortion while caring for women who have been wounded by abortionists. We can preach against spiritual pride and arrogance while loving self-righteous snobs.

The world thinks that the only way to love people is to tolerate and approve of their sinful, self-destructive lifestyles. We Christians know better. We have seen in the Gospels that Jesus was a friend of sinners, yet He never approved of their sin. Jesus was a friend to the woman caught in adultery, but He told her to go and leave her life of sin (John 8:11). Jesus was a friend to Zacchaeus, the crooked tax collector, but when the message of Jesus convicted him, he repented and repaid those he had cheated—*four times over* (Luke 19:8).

Authentic Christian love tells the truth and confronts sin. The world will say we are judgmental and unloving if we confront sin. Let's dare to be slandered as "unloving" while we dare to love as Jesus loves.

THE ANTICHRIST AND THE MAHDI

Is the Christian faith the only religion that teaches about the Last Days? No. In fact, the three largest monotheistic religions—Judaism, Christianity, and Islam—all devote a great deal of attention to eschatology, the study of end-times prophecies. There are startling parallels between the prophetic teachings of these three religions:

Jerusalem. The end-times prophecies of all three religions center largely on events in and around Jerusalem and the Mount of Olives.

Signs Preceding Judgment. In all three religions, there are prophetic signs pointing to the Last Days and Final Judgment. Jesus speaks of these signs in Matthew 24:4–28.

The Messiah. All three religions predict the coming of the Messiah. In Judaism, the Messiah will restore the kingdom of Israel and God will be Israel's King (Zechariah 14). In Christianity, Jesus the Messiah will return to earth, defeat the Antichrist, and rule over the Messianic kingdom (Matthew 19:28; Revelation 20:4–6). In Islam, Jesus is called Isa, and He is a prophet and the *Masîh* (the Islamic Messiah) who will one day return to help the Imam Mahdi defeat the *al-Masih ad-Dajjal* (the Islamic Antichrist).

Final War. In Judaism, the Messiah leads Israel to victory over Israel's enemies. In Christianity, Satan instigates the final conflict, the Battle of Armageddon. Islam also features a final battle, and like Judaism and Christianity, makes reference to the nations of Gog and Magog (*Yajuj* and *Majuj*; Quran 18:94–100).

Sheikh Hisham Kabbani, a Lebanese-American Sufi scholar, observed, "Jews are waiting for the Messiah, Christians are waiting for Jesus, and Muslims are waiting for both the Mahdi and Jesus. All religions describe them as men coming to save the world."[5]

Despite these similarities, there are major differences between the prophecies of the Old and New Testaments and the prophetic passages of the Quran. The central figure of Islamic eschatology is called the Imam Mahdi (*Mahdi* means "the Guided One"). Muslims view the Imam Mahdi as a savior who will lead a revolution to establish a global empire, the final Caliphate. The Mahdi will rule the earth as the rightful successor to the Prophet Muhammad.

Sunni Muslims and Shia Muslims have differing views regarding the Mahdi. The Sunnis view the Mahdi as a righteous, wise, and divinely inspired human being but do not view him as a supernatural being. They believe he will be born, live a natural life span, and die like any other human being.

The largest sect of Shia Muslims (the Twelver Shia) takes a more mythological view of the Mahdi. They believe the Mahdi was Muhammad ibn Hasan al-Mahdī, who was born in 869, became an imam (religious leader) at age five, and is still alive today, more than eleven centuries later. They believe he underwent two periods of "occultation" (being miraculously hidden from the world), and will remain in occultation until he returns to lead the faithful and punish the infidels just before the Judgment Day.

Dr. Samuel Shahid, director of Islamic studies at Southwestern Baptist Theological Seminary, observes that the Mahdi of Shia Islam "is the embodiment of the earnest longing and hope of the Shiites who have been oppressed and persecuted throughout the course of history." Dr. Shahid describes the mythological nature of the Shiite Mahdi:

> The Shiites believe that when the Mahdi reappears from his great occultation, he will recover the original book of Psalms from the lake of Tiberius, the Torah and the Gospel, the Ark of the Covenant, the Tablets of Moses and his Staff, and the Ring of Solomon, from a cave in Antioch. . . . The Mahdi will conquer the world and destroy all the infidels . . . [and] take over every city, even Jerusalem, that Alexander the Great vanquished, and [he will] reform them. That will gratify the hearts of the people of Islam. . . .
>
> The universal Islamic community he establishes is not based on peace or love. It is an earthly militant kingdom under the banner of Islam in which people either will accept the Shiite type of Islam, or will be killed.[6]

Here's one of the most troubling aspects of Islamic eschatology: Islam's "savior," the Mahdi, bears a striking resemblance not to the biblical Christ but to the biblical Antichrist. Why would Satan's masterpiece, the Antichrist, so closely resemble the Islamic Mahdi? I believe it's because Satan knows the Bible. He is preparing the followers of Islam to look upon the Antichrist and see him as their long-prophesied Imam Mahdi. For centuries, Satan has been preparing the Muslim people to receive the Antichrist as their savior.

Muslims believe the Mahdi will appear when Jesus (Isa) returns. Yes, Muslims believe in Jesus, but not as their Savior and not as the Son of God. To Muslims, Jesus is a great prophet, and they call Him the *Masîh* (Messiah). They deny that Jesus died on the cross. Most important, they revere the Mahdi (who has all the biblical earmarks of the Antichrist) above Isa (Jesus).

In *Al Mahdi and the End of Time*, Egyptian Islamic scholars Muhammad Ibn Izzat and Muhammad Arif describe in vivid terms what the coming of the Mahdi means to Muslims:

> The Mahdi will be victorious and eradicate those pigs and dogs and the idols of this time so that there will once more be [a] caliphate based on prophethood. . . .
>
> Jerusalem will be the location of the rightly-guided caliphate and the centre of Islamic rule, which will be headed by Imam al-Mahdi. . . .
>
> That will abolish the leadership of the Jews, who direct the world from within the Masonic circles, and put an end to the domination of the shaytans [satans or demons] who spit evil into people and cause corruption in the earth, making them slaves of false idols and ruling the world by laws other than the *Shari'a* [Islamic law] of the Lord of the worlds. It will be the Day of Salvation from this Era of Ignorance.[7]

These Islamic scholars state that non-Muslims ("pigs and dogs") will be defeated and exterminated by the Mahdi. The Mahdi will overthrow Jewish governance of Jerusalem. (These scholars reflect a common Islamic conspiracy theory that the Jews are implicated with the Freemasons in a secret plot for world domination.) The arrival of the Mahdi, the scholars claim, will usher in the "Day of Salvation." The book of Revelation, however, says that the arrival of the Antichrist will trigger the Great Tribulation.

According to Islamic prophecy, Jesus will descend in Syria, east of Damascus, and He will assist the Mahdi in establishing the final Caliphate over the entire earth. At the end of the Mahdi's rule, there will be a Day of Judgment.

When you study Islamic eschatology, you discover that the Mahdi has all of the power and authority of the Antichrist. Both the Mahdi and the Antichrist are said to possess supreme political and religious authority. Both the Mahdi and the Antichrist will be worshipped as the head of a one-world religion. Like the Antichrist, the Mahdi will establish his capital in Jerusalem, and he will rule the world from that holy city.

The Bible says that the Antichrist will target Jews and Christians for destruction; Islamic eschatology says the Mahdi will wage war against Jews and Christians. Those who oppose the Antichrist will be executed; those who oppose the Mahdi will be executed. Iranian religious leader Ayatullah Ibrahim Amini writes that the Mahdi "will offer the religion of Islam to the non-believers [Jews, Christians, and other non-Muslims]. Anyone who accepts that call will be saved from being killed. All those who refuse to accept Islam will be killed."[8]

Daniel 9:27 tells us that the Antichrist "will confirm a covenant with many for one 'seven.' In the middle of the 'seven' he will put an end to sacrifice and offering. And at the temple he will set up an abomination that causes desolation, until the end that is decreed is poured out on him." The "covenant with many" refers to a covenant with many nations. Clearly, Israel will be a party to this covenant. Daniel tells us that halfway through the seven-year term of the covenant, the Antichrist will break the covenant, and this act of treachery will have catastrophic implications for Israel. The Antichrist will put an end to temple sacrifices and set up "an abomination that causes desolation" in the temple.

Islam's Hadith literature also speaks of a seven-year covenant the Mahdi (or "al-Mahdi") makes with the "Romans"—that is, the nations of Europe. Islamic scholar Dr. Abul Hassan explains:

> Al-Mahdi is said to be one who will initiate Islam's fourth and final treaty between the "Romans" and the Muslims. Al-Mahdi will make this treaty for a period of seven years! In a Hadith, Prophet Muhammad (peace be upon him) said: "There will be four peace agreements between you and the Romans. The fourth will be mediated through a person who will be from the progeny of Hazrat Aaron (the brother of Moses) and will be upheld for seven years. . . . It appears that the period of this seven year peace agreement will likewise be the period of the Mahdi's reign.[9]

There are a number of important points in Dr. Hassan's statement. First, just as the Antichrist will make a covenant with "many," the Mahdi will make a covenant with the "Romans," or nations of Europe. Second, both the Antichrist in Daniel and the Mahdi will make a covenant lasting for seven years. Third, Dr. Hassan notes that the term of this seven-year peace agreement will coincide with the seven years of the Mahdi's reign; the book of Revelation tells us that the Antichrist will reign for seven years.

There is one notable discrepancy between Daniel's prophecy about the Antichrist and Muhammad's prophecy about the Mahdi: Daniel says that the Antichrist will break the treaty halfway through the seven-year period. Muhammad's prophecy in the Hadith says nothing about breaking the agreement after three and a half years. Of course, if the Mahdi *is* the Antichrist, he won't want to reveal his plans in advance.

Muhammad is quoted in the Hadith as saying that this seven-year treaty will be mediated through a descendant of "Hazrat Aaron" (Arabic for "His Holiness Aaron"). Aaron was the older brother of Moses and—this is significant!—Aaron was also the *first high priest* in Israel. Today, no Jewish person can trace his or her ancestry back to Aaron. So this "progeny" of Aaron will be a descendant in the sense of Aaron's priestly office. When you combine the Daniel prophecy with the Islamic prophecy, they seem to be saying that the high priest of the reconstructed temple of Jerusalem will serve as the mediator of this agreement—and the Antichrist will break the agreement halfway through the Great Tribulation and will defile the temple with the "abomination."

In another passage of the Hadith, Abu Sa'id al-Khudri quotes Muhammad as saying, "The Mahdi . . . will fill the earth with fairness and justice as it was filled with oppression and injustice, and he will rule for seven years."[10] Again, the length of the Mahdi's rule and the length of the Antichrist's reign are the same—seven years.

In *Al Mahdi and the End of Time*, Muhammad Ibn Izzat and Muhammad Arif observe that Revelation 6:2 says, "I looked, and there before me was a white horse! Its rider held a bow, and he was given a crown, and he rode out as a conqueror bent on conquest." As we saw earlier, this rider on a white horse appears to be a false man of peace, Satan's counterfeit, the Antichrist. And who do these two Islamic scholars say the rider on the white horse will be? They write, "It is clear that this man is the Mahdi who will ride the white horse and judge by the Qur'an."[11] So the Antichrist of Revelation is identified by Islamic scholars as the Mahdi.

When Muslims call for a worldwide Caliphate, they are calling for the coming of the Mahdi, the long-prophesied "final Caliph" of Islam. When he appears, every Muslim on earth will be required to follow him. Shaykh Muhammad Hisham Kabbani writes that Muhammad said of the Mahdi (as quoted by the Hadith narrator Thawban), "If you see him, go and give him your allegiance, even if you have to crawl over ice, because he is the Viceregent (*Khalifa*) of Allah, the Mahdi."[12]

There seems little doubt that Satan is preparing Muslims to accept the Mahdi as their leader. On close examination, the Mahdi seems indistinguishable from the Antichrist. When this counterfeit "savior" the Bible calls the Antichrist arises to impose his bloody reign upon the world, Muslims will be well prepared to welcome him as their long-promised Mahdi. And they will follow him to hell itself.

Today, there are two Islamic regimes in the Middle East. There is the Shia Islamic Republic of Iran, and there is the self-proclaimed Sunni caliphate that calls itself the Islamic State, or ISIS. The political policies and ideologies of both regimes are driven by an extreme end-times theology. The leaders of both regimes believe they have been chosen by Allah to plunge the world into global war. They plan to destroy Israel and the United States, and thereby hasten the return of the Mahdi. They do not hesitate to use torture, slaughter, and terror to achieve their goal of uniting the world under Sharia law and the Mahdi's global caliphate.

The ceaseless campaign of terror that Islamic extremists wage against the West is a foretaste of the future reign of the Antichrist. As Jesus foretold, "For then there will be great distress, unequaled from the beginning of the world until now—and never to be equaled again" (Matthew 24:21).

THE RISE OF THE FALSE PROPHET

In the final seven verses of Revelation 13, John reveals a second beast. John describes the rise of the second beast:

> Then I saw a second beast, coming out of the earth. It had two horns like a lamb, but it spoke like a dragon. It exercised all the authority of the first beast on its behalf, and made the earth and its inhabitants worship the first beast, whose fatal wound had been healed. And it performed great signs, even causing fire to come down from heaven to the earth in full view of the people. Because of the signs it was given power to perform on behalf of the first beast,

it deceived the inhabitants of the earth. It ordered them to set up an image in honor of the beast who was wounded by the sword and yet lived. The second beast was given power to give breath to the image of the first beast, so that the image could speak and cause all who refused to worship the image to be killed. It also forced all people, great and small, rich and poor, free and slave, to receive a mark on their right hands or on their foreheads, so that they could not buy or sell unless they had the mark, which is the name of the beast or the number of its name. (vv. 11–17)

The first Beast arose from the sea of humanity. The second beast will rise from the earth, and he will ensure that the people of earth worship the first Beast. The second beast is often referred to as "the False Prophet," because he has the appearance of a lamb—meaning he will look and sound like Christ. People will see him as a man of God, a divine spiritual leader. Some people will even mistake him for Jesus, the Lamb of God. But the False Prophet will enforce the worship of the Antichrist. He will perform false miracles by the power of Satan, and even call down fire from the sky.

According to Islamic eschatology, Isa (Jesus) will assist the Mahdi, just as the Bible says that the False Prophet will assist the Antichrist to establish his global empire. This is not a coincidence. Once again, Satan knows the Scriptures better than we do. Satan knows every verse of the Bible, and he is preparing the Islamic world to recognize the Antichrist as the Mahdi and the False Prophet as Isa.

John writes that the False Prophet will have power to perform signs and wonders on behalf of the Antichrist, to deceive the people of the earth. The False Prophet will order the people to set up an image, a statue, in honor of the Antichrist.

This conforms to the prophecy of Daniel 9:27, where the angel Gabriel says that in the middle of the seven years of the Tribulation, the Antichrist will put an end to sacrifices and offerings at the temple. An image will be set up in the temple to honor the Antichrist—"an abomination that causes desolation." And the False Prophet will have power from Satan to cause the image of the Antichrist to move and speak. What will the image say? It will give an order that all who refuse to worship the image will be executed.

Everyone on earth must receive the mark of the beast on their right hands or foreheads. Those who refuse the mark will not be able to buy or sell. Imagine if the government forbade you to hold a job, to own a business, or to buy food, clothing, or a home. What would you do? What would you eat? How would you feed your family? What about welfare? Sorry, you don't have the mark. No government assistance for you. Would you go to a religious charity for help? What religious charity? There is only one religion—the religion of the Antichrist—and any who oppose that religion must be eliminated.

The last verse of Revelation 13 has baffled Bible scholars for centuries: "This calls for wisdom. Let the person who has insight calculate the number of the beast, for it is the number of a man. That number is 666" (v. 18). The number 666 has terrified superstitious people. Some think that if 666 is the "number of the Beast," then it must be "unlucky." Many people have refused to accept a telephone number or license plate that contains 666.

In 1988, as Ronald Reagan was preparing to leave the White House, he purchased a home in the Bel Air section of Los Angeles. The address was 666 St. Cloud Road. He had the street number changed to 668 to avoid the number of the Beast.[13]

People have tried to use the number 666 to figure out the identity of the Antichrist. But I don't believe that number is a secret code or a hidden key to the Antichrist's identity. As we have seen, the Bible uses the number 7 to represent the perfection and completeness of God. If something appears perfect but it isn't of God, it's not the number 7—it's the number 6. It falls short of God's perfection.

If 7 represents Christ, then 6 represents Satan. If 7 represents perfection, then 6 represents fallenness—a wickedness that pretends to be perfect. If the holy Trinity of God (the Father, Son, and Holy Spirit) may be thought of as 777, then the unholy trinity of Satan, the Antichrist, and the False Prophet may be thought of as 666. There are other possible explanations of 666. This is merely my opinion. Someday, after these prophecies are fulfilled, we will know beyond any doubt what each symbol means.

Meanwhile, I don't want anyone to have a superstitious fear of that number. If your name is written in the book of life, then you have nothing to fear from the Antichrist. Our names are written in the blood of the Lamb of God, Jesus Himself. Nothing can erase your name from His Book. When you know that Jesus is your Lord and Savior, you have the peace of knowing He is always with you.

When He comes to take His followers home, He will receive you with open arms.

Once, when I was preaching on the book of Revelation, a twelve-year-old girl in the audience heard me say that the False Prophet would force everyone to receive the mark of the beast—and she heard that in heaven, we will see the face of Jesus, and His name will be on our foreheads (Revelation 22:4).

Afterward, she went home and wrote one word on her forehead: JESUS. When she came out of her room, her parents asked her why she had written it. "Because," she said, "I don't want the Antichrist to have his name on my forehead. I want to belong to Jesus."

This young lady is wise beyond her years. May you and I follow her example, write the name of Jesus on our foreheads, and boldly proclaim His name to the world.

FOUR

THE REIGN AND FALL OF THE ANTICHRIST

IF YOU EVER VISIT the reading room in the rotunda of the Library of Congress, look above the pillars that support the dome. You'll see a series of plaques with quotations in gold lettering. One plaque reads:

> One God, one law, one element
> and one far-off divine event
> to which the whole creation moves.

Thousands of people pass through that room every year, but few pause to consider those words. They're from the epilogue to Alfred Lord Tennyson's "In Memoriam." The poet is reflecting on the brevity of this life and the inevitable fall of civilizations. He reminds us that the world is moving toward one God-ordained event that will bring history to a close.

Someday, even America will be no more. The whole world will come under the domination of a world leader known as the Antichrist. Yet even the empire of the Antichrist will not endure for long. With the destruction of the Antichrist and his dominion, God will bring history to a close.

The reign of the Antichrist corresponds to the period we call the Great Tribulation. The Great Tribulation is not described in one section of Revelation. The events of the Tribulation are spread across the book of Revelation, especially in the judgments of Revelation 4–11 and the symbols of Revelation 12–19 (the woman and child, the Dragon, the two beasts, the great harlot, and the Lamb). The book unfolds as a series of themes rather than a sequence of chronological events.

In the book of Revelation, we witness the culmination of history as God pours out His judgment against sin during the Tribulation. Though these scenes are disturbing, we should not fear the future. Rather, we should spiritually prepare ourselves to face the future. The central message of Revelation is not the end of this world but the glorious unveiling of the new heaven and the new earth.

The book of Revelation does not leave us in despair. It lifts our spirits and ignites our passion to witness for Christ. I'm more excited today about God's prophetic Word than at any other time in my life. These are great times for sharing the saving knowledge of our victorious Lord Jesus. I'm grateful to be living in these exciting days.

THE TITLE DEED TO PLANET EARTH

As we look at the reign and fall of the Antichrist, let's pause and consider an event that takes place in heaven just before the beginning of the Great Tribulation. This event is described in Revelation 4 and 5.

John looks and sees a door standing open in heaven, and a voice like a trumpet invites him to enter the throne room of heaven. Someone sits on the throne, and a rainbow encircles the throne. Before the throne stand twenty-four elders dressed in white. There are flashes of lightning and rumblings of thunder, and before the throne is a sea of glass, as clear as crystal. There are creatures around the throne, singing praises to God.

At the beginning of Revelation 5, John sees that the One upon the throne holds a scroll in His right hand. The scroll is rolled up and sealed with seven seals. John weeps because no one can be found who is worthy to break the seals and open the scroll.

Clearly, the scroll contains an important secret. I believe the secret hidden within the scroll is the key to the book of Revelation. The secret contained in the scroll is so important that John weeps uncontrollably when no one is found worthy to open it. The scroll contains vital information about the future of the human race.

I'm going to venture an opinion about this scroll. I can't prove my opinion is correct, but it is consistent with Scripture. I believe John wept because he knew that the scroll was the title deed to planet Earth. I base this view on an incident in Jeremiah 32. At that time, the kingdom of Judah lay devastated and defeated. The Babylonians had Jerusalem under siege. The city was gripped by panic and the people were dying of famine. Soon the kingdom would fall and the slaughter would begin.

In the midst of this calamity, the Lord told Jeremiah to buy a piece of land. Jeremiah couldn't understand God's reasons, but he obeyed and bought the land from his cousin Hanamel. Then he placed the title deed for the land in a clay jar for safekeeping. That sealed deed represents God's promise to Israel. God had promised that after seventy years, He would lead Israel out of exile in Babylon and back into the promised land.

I believe John, in Revelation, knew that the scroll with the seven seals was also a title deed. It was a symbol of God's promise to the human race. God gave the title deed for planet Earth to Adam, but Adam lost the deed to Satan through his disobedience at the Fall.

Satan has been running planet Earth since the time of Adam, and Satan will continue to be "the god of this world" (2 Corinthians 4:4 KJV) until the glorious appearing of Jesus Christ. John wept when no one was found worthy to open the seals because it meant that Satan still ruled planet Earth.

But in Revelation 5:5, one of the elders says, "Do not weep! See, the Lion of the tribe of Judah, the Root of David, has triumphed. He is able to open the scroll and its seven seals."

Then John sees the Lamb who was slain, appearing as if He has been sacrificed. The Lamb has seven horns, seven eyes, and seven spirits. As we have seen, the number seven speaks of perfection and completion. The seven horns speak of the Lamb's perfect power. The seven eyes speak of His all-knowing wisdom. The seven spirits depict the sevenfold ministry of the Holy Spirit.

The Lamb, of course, is Jesus. He has conquered death and won back the title deed of planet Earth from Satan. All the creatures of heaven praise Him:

You are worthy to take the scroll
and to open its seals,
because you were slain,
and with your blood you purchased for God
persons from every tribe and language and people
and nation.
You have made them to be a kingdom and priests to serve
our God,
and they will reign on the earth. (Revelation 5:9–10)

Notice that one of the elders called the Lamb of God by another name: "the Lion of the tribe of Judah" (Revelation 5:5). The Lamb who was slain is also the Lion who executes judgment. If your sins are covered by the blood of the Lamb, then you need not fear the Lion. The Lion will judge you based on what you have done with the Lamb. Did you receive the Lamb as your Lord and Savior? Or did you ignore Him?

If the Lamb is not your Savior, then the Lion will be your Judge.

UNLEASHING THE GREAT TRIBULATION

The most somber part of Revelation is the opening of the seals. When the Lamb breaks the first seal, the Great Tribulation begins—and the Antichrist steps onto the world stage. In all the bloody history of the human race, this will be the darkest and bloodiest of all. The Tribulation was foretold in Daniel 9 by the angel Gabriel:

He instructed me and said to me, "Daniel, I have now come to give you insight and understanding. As soon as you began to pray, a word went out, which I have come to tell you, for you are highly esteemed. Therefore, consider the word and understand the vision:

"Seventy 'sevens' are decreed for your people and your holy city to finish transgression, to put an end to sin, to atone for wickedness, to bring in everlasting righteousness, to seal up vision and prophecy and to anoint the Most Holy Place.

"Know and understand this: From the time the word goes out to restore and rebuild Jerusalem until the Anointed One, the ruler, comes, there will be seven 'sevens,' and sixty-two 'sevens.' It will be rebuilt with streets and a trench, but in times of trouble. After the sixty-two 'sevens,' the Anointed One will be put to death and will have nothing. The people of the ruler who will come will destroy the city and the sanctuary. The end will come like a flood: War will continue until the end, and desolations have been decreed. He will confirm a covenant with many for one 'seven.' In the middle of the 'seven' he will put an end to sacrifice and offering. And at the temple he will set up an abomination that causes desolation, until the end that is decreed is poured out on him." (vv. 22–27)

The first person to unlock the mystery of these verses was Sir Robert Anderson, a high-ranking police commissioner at Scotland Yard. In his book *The Coming Prince* (1894), Anderson worked out, with mathematical precision, the meaning of this prophecy. Anderson saw that the seven "sevens" of years plus sixty-two "sevens" of years equaled sixty-nine "sevens" of years. Sixty-nine times seven equals 483.

Notice that phrase: "from the time the word goes out to restore and rebuild Jerusalem." Anderson realized it referred to the decree of King Artaxerxes I of Persia, who ordered the rebuilding of Jerusalem. Using information from both the book of Nehemiah and secular history, Anderson determined that the decree was issued on March 14, 445 BC (the first day of the Hebrew month of Nisan). So the prophecy predicted that, from March 14, 445 BC until the Anointed One, the Messiah, came as a ruler, would be a span of 483 years. Using a 360-day calendar—the same calendar Israel used in Daniel's time—Anderson calculated that 483 years equals 173,880 days. Anderson counted the number of days from Artaxerxes' decree to Palm Sunday, April 6, AD 32—and it came to *precisely* 173,880 days.

The prophecy of Gabriel in Daniel 9 predicted *the exact date* of the Lord's triumphant entry into Jerusalem as Israel's King. Isn't it amazing that the proof of this ancient prophecy lay undiscovered until Sir Robert Anderson did his computations in the 1890s?

Still more amazing, Gabriel told Daniel: "After the sixty-two 'sevens,' the Anointed One will be put to death and will have nothing" (Daniel 9:26). Less than a week after that Palm Sunday, Jesus was crucified.

And there's more: the angel Gabriel goes on to say, "The people of the ruler who will come will destroy the city and the sanctuary" (v. 26). This prophecy was fulfilled in AD 70 when the Roman army, commanded by General Titus (who later became emperor of Rome, "the ruler who will come"), conquered Jerusalem and destroyed the temple. Centuries later, Jesus also predicted the destruction of the temple:

> Jesus left the temple and was walking away when his disciples came up to him to call his attention to its buildings. "Do you see all these things?" he asked. "Truly I tell you, not one stone here will be left on another; every one will be thrown down." (Matthew 24:1–2)

But there's more to Gabriel's prophecy. The angel went on to tell Daniel about another seven-year period of prophetic history:

> The end will come like a flood: War will continue until the end, and desolations have been decreed. He will confirm a covenant with many for one 'seven.' In the middle of the 'seven' he will put an end to sacrifice and offering. And at the temple he will set up an abomination that causes desolation, until the end that is decreed is poured out on him. (Daniel 9:26-27)

Here, Gabriel tells Daniel of a seven-year period that is separate from the earlier "sevens." Today, Gabriel's prophecy of the triumphant entry and death of the Messiah has been fulfilled. His prophecy of the destruction of Jerusalem has been fulfilled. But his prophecy of the seven years of the Antichrist's reign has *not* yet been fulfilled. This seven-year time of tribulation lies in our future.

THE RECONSTRUCTED TEMPLE IN JERUSALEM

As you study the seven-year period of the Great Tribulation, you find that the prophecies of Daniel, Jesus, and the book of Revelation are absolutely consistent. They all refer to the reconstructed temple in Jerusalem. The prophecy of the reconstructed temple is implied yet undeniable.

The angel Gabriel tells Daniel that enemies will "destroy the city and the sanctuary" (9:26), yet just a few sentences later, he says, "at the temple [the Antichrist] will set up an abomination that causes desolation" (v. 27). Similarly, Jesus tells His disciples that the temple will be destroyed (Matthew 24:2)—then He, too, tells them that the Antichrist will set up the abomination of desolation in the temple (v. 15). So, according to some interpretations of Scripture, the temple must be rebuilt.

In Revelation 11:1, God tells John to take a measuring rod and measure the temple. Some Bible scholars think this refers to a literal temple in Jerusalem. But no Jewish temple has stood on the Temple Mount in Jerusalem since the destruction of the second temple by the Romans in AD 70 (the first temple was Solomon's temple, which was destroyed by the Babylonians). What stands on the Temple Mount today? Two Islamic edifices, the Al-Aqsa Mosque (the third holiest site in Islam) and the Dome of the Rock, the golden-capped shrine that is one of Jerusalem's most famous landmarks.

The Temple Mount is a sacred site to Jews, Muslims, and Christians. Muslims call the walled compound atop the Mount the Noble Sanctuary. In that compound, the Muslims built the Al-Aqsa Mosque in 705 (it has been destroyed and rebuilt several times). Muslims built the Dome of the Rock in 691, constructing the shrine around the foundation stone, which the Jews believe was the site of the Holy of Holies of the second temple—and the very spot where Abraham bound Isaac to sacrifice him. When both Jews and Muslims claim one rock as their holy site, there will be trouble.

After the Muslim warrior Saladin defeated the Crusaders and recaptured Palestine in 1187, the Muslims banned all non-Muslim prayer on the Temple Mount—a ban that is in force to this day. Lately, growing numbers of Orthodox Jews visit the Temple Mount, walking barefoot on the stones as a sign of respect to God, and praying under their breath in defiance of Muslim law. If they are caught praying, they are forcibly removed from the site.

Meanwhile, Jews are demanding the freedom to pray alongside Muslims on the Temple Mount. Some are laying plans and raising funds for a new temple, crafting ritual utensils of gold and silver, and hand-stitching priestly vestments. Israeli cattle breeders hope to produce an unblemished red heifer—a young cow that has never calved and is red from nose to tail—to be sacrificed in accordance with God's command in Numbers 19:2. An unblemished red heifer has not been seen in Israel in nearly two thousand years, but many Israelis hope to sacrifice a red heifer as part of the restored temple worship.

Ever since the Israelis captured the Old City of Jerusalem during the Six-Day War in 1967, the Temple Mount has been the most fiercely disputed piece of real estate in the world. In 1990, a group of Israelis attempted to lay a cornerstone for a new Jewish Temple and rioting broke out, killing twenty-two Palestinians.

In 2000, Israeli leader Ariel Sharon visited the Temple Mount and a violent uprising broke out. Over five years, that uprising (the Second Intifada) killed three thousand Palestinians and one thousand Israelis.

Muslim Palestinians are angry about Jewish plans to build a third temple where the Dome of the Rock now stands. Mohammad Ahmed Hussein, the Grand Mufti of Jerusalem's Muslim community, said, "No one but Muslims are allowed to perform any kind of prayers at Al-Aqsa [meaning the entire Al-Aqsa compound]. Jewish prayer at Al-Aqsa is . . . an aggression."[1]

Meanwhile, Yehuda Glick, an American-born rabbi who leads Israel's Temple Mount Heritage Foundation, has vowed, "The Third Temple, which will be a house of prayer for all nations, will be built very soon."[2]

At Jerusalem's Shalem College, hundreds of Jewish students study the ancient rituals of sacrifice and laws of Passover. They wear priestly vestments, slaughter sacrificial lambs, and sprinkle blood on the altar. They are practicing to perform these rituals in the future temple. The director of the program, Rabbi Yehoshua Friedman, anticipates a fully operating temple where hundreds of priests will carry out the ancient temple sacrifices.

Only one problem stands in the way—the Dome of the Rock, which currently occupies that site. One person involved in the temple rebuilding effort put it this way: "If not for the problem of the Dome of the Rock, they would build the temple today."[3]

The prophecies of Daniel and Jesus in Revelation make it clear that a third temple will be built. And it is equally clear that the third temple cannot be built without enraging the Muslim world.

MEASURING THE TEMPLE OF GOD

Returning to Revelation 11, we see that God told John to measure the temple of God. It may be that God literally wants John to measure the physical temple of Jerusalem that will exist during the Great Tribulation. But there may be another explanation for God's command to John: He may be telling John to draw a measuring line around God's people. As Paul wrote, "Don't you know that you yourselves are God's temple and that God's Spirit dwells in your midst?" (1 Corinthians 3:16). I believe that John's measuring of the temple in Revelation 11 symbolizes God placing His protective boundary around believers.

To measure is to define limits. John's measuring line draws a boundary around God's people. Satan and his fallen angels cannot touch us, because God has sealed us and has measured out a boundary line around us.

Persecutors cannot destroy the true temple of God, because the temple is the church of Jesus Christ, the body of believers. Persecutors may be able to enter the outer courts of the temple, but not the inner courts. We are safe within God's sanctuary, inside His measured boundary line of protection.

Whether John's measurement refers to the physical temple or to the figurative temple composed of all believers, we know that the temple will be built. During the Great Tribulation, the people of Israel will offer sacrifices to God according to the Old Testament pattern.

And halfway through the Great Tribulation, the Antichrist will set up the abomination of desolation in the sanctuary of the temple in Jerusalem.

THE FALSE PROPHET AND
THE ANOINTED WITNESSES

In Revelation 11, we meet two witnesses who proclaim the gospel one last time. John presents them in symbols that echo Old Testament prophecy:

> "And I will appoint my two witnesses, and they will prophesy for 1,260 days, clothed in sackcloth." They are "the two olive trees" and the two lampstands, and "they stand before the Lord of the earth." If anyone tries to harm them, fire comes from their mouths and devours their enemies. This is how anyone who wants to harm them must die. They have power to shut up the heavens so that it will not rain during the time they are prophesying; and they have power to turn the waters into blood and to strike the earth with every kind of plague as often as they want. (vv. 3–6)

These two witnesses will prophesy for 1,260 days, which is exactly three and a half years, according to the Hebrew 360-day calendar. The symbol of two olive trees and the two lampstands comes from the book of Zechariah:

> Then I asked the angel, "What are these two olive trees on the right and the left of the lampstand?" . . .
>
> He replied, "Do you not know what these are?"
>
> "No, my lord," I said.
>
> So he said, "These are the two who are anointed to serve the Lord of all the earth." (4:11, 13–14)

Olive oil was used for anointing, so the olive trees stand for two men who are anointed to proclaim God's truth. The two lampstands symbolize those who shine God's truth into a darkened world.

Though the Scriptures do not identify these witnesses by name, they are almost certainly Moses and Elijah. In the Gospels, Moses and Elijah met with Jesus on the Mount of Transfiguration: "Two men, Moses and Elijah, appeared in glorious splendor, talking with Jesus" (Luke 9:30). In Revelation 11, these two witnesses have all the earmarks of Moses and Elijah. They possess the same supernatural powers Moses and Elijah had in the Old Testament—the power to call down fire, stop the rain, turn water to blood, and strike the earth with plagues.

Some Bible scholars believe Moses and Elijah will literally return in the flesh in those days. Others suggest that these figures symbolize faithful believers in the Last Days who will perform miracles and prophesy in God's name. God will give these witnesses a supernatural anointing to proclaim His truth, and they will act in complete unity. They will prophesy together, suffer together, and die together. They will be raised together and ascend to heaven together.

Now when they have finished their testimony, the beast that comes up from the Abyss will attack them, and overpower and kill them. Their bodies will lie in the public square of the great city—which is figuratively called Sodom and Egypt—where also their Lord was crucified. For three and a half days some from every people, tribe, language and nation will gaze on their bodies and refuse them burial. The inhabitants of the earth will gloat over them and will celebrate by sending each other gifts, because these two prophets had tormented those who live on the earth.

But after the three and a half days the breath of life from God entered them, and they stood on their feet, and terror struck those who saw them. Then they heard a loud voice from heaven saying to them, "Come up here." And they went up to heaven in a cloud, while their enemies looked on. (Revelation 11:7–12)

These two witnesses have a ministry on earth that lasts for three and a half years, right to the midpoint of the Great Tribulation. Notice that this is the same point in time when Daniel and Jesus predict that the abomination of desolation will be set up to defile the temple. At that same time, "the beast that comes up from the Abyss"—this is the *second* beast (the False Prophet)—"will attack them, and overpower and kill them."

The corrupt government of the Antichrist leaves the corpses of the witnesses in the public square of the city. There may be two corpses, belonging to Moses and Elijah—or, if the "two witnesses" symbolize many anointed witnesses, there could be hundreds or thousands of corpses. The entire world will see these bodies in the public square—perhaps by means of television, the Internet, and smartphones.

John says that this takes place in the great city where the Lord was crucified—Jerusalem—yet he also says that the city "is figuratively called Sodom and Egypt." These symbols tell us a lot about what the kind of place Jerusalem will be when it is the capital city of the Antichrist's global empire. Jerusalem will be like Sodom, a place of wide-open corruption, violence, and sexual immorality. And Jerusalem will be like Egypt, a place of oppression and bondage. Just as Jerusalem crucified Christ, so the godless empire of the Antichrist will crucify His followers.

What did these witnesses do to warrant execution? They preached God's message. They testified to God's truth. By simply speaking the truth, John says, these two witnesses tormented the people of the earth. We already see a rising intolerance toward the truth today. If you speak God's truth, people will try to shut you up. They will slander you. They will try to get you fired from your job. Some of the most intolerant people you'll ever meet are those who preach "tolerance." Yes, they gladly tolerate any form of immorality or abortion or false doctrines—but they cannot tolerate God's truth.

The people of the world rejoice over the death of these witnesses. They even celebrate a satanic anti-Christmas, exchanging gifts to celebrate these deaths. When ungodly people feel the conviction of sin, they frequently get angry. They will hate you and try to destroy you. An old Arabian proverb says, "He who would tell the truth should have one foot in the stirrup." In other words, if you tell people the truth, you'd better have an escape plan, because they will come after you.

In May 2012, scientist Mark Armitage of California State University at Northridge made an amazing discovery. While working at a fossil dig in Montana, he discovered one of the largest triceratops horns ever found. He brought it back to California and conducted microscopic examination of the horn—and the microscope revealed well-preserved soft tissue. Armitage is a Young Earth Creationist, and a fossil with soft tissue lends support to his belief that dinosaurs died in the Genesis flood about four thousand years ago, not sixty-eight million years ago as evolutionists claim.

In February 2013, Armitage published a paper in *Acta Histochemica*, a peer-reviewed journal of cell and tissue research. Armitage reported his findings without drawing any conclusion about the age of the fossil. He made no reference to creationism or the Flood or the Bible. Two weeks after the paper appeared in print, the university fired him.[4] He was fired for simply reporting the scientific facts.

Armitage sued to get his job back. Court documents show that a university official told him, "We are not going to tolerate your religion in this department!"[5]

Firing someone because of his or her religion is illegal in America. Attempting to bury scientific evidence and silence free speech violates all principles of scientific ethics. So far, Armitage's firing stands. We can expect *more* persecution of Christians for the "crime" of speaking the truth in days to come.

Truth always provokes hostility. The truth can cost you your career. A day is coming when it may cost you your life. Don't let threats or intimidation silence you. Speak the truth. Provoke a confrontation. Lay out your evidence and demand a verdict.

Don't accept the namby-pamby nonsense that Jesus was a "good moral teacher." C. S. Lewis observed that by claiming to be God, Jesus made it clear that He was either a liar, a lunatic, or the Lord God.[6] Jesus has not left any other option open to us.

I once heard an English bishop say, "When the apostle Paul came into a town, he either incited a riot or triggered a revival. When I go into a town, they give me a high tea. In all truthfulness, I don't want high tea. I would settle for either revival or a riot. At least the riot would prove I had proclaimed God's truth without compromise."

If you compromise the message of Jesus, the world will love you. But if you proclaim Jesus and His gospel without compromise, the world will hate you. Proclaim it anyway, just as the witnesses in Revelation 11 proclaimed the gospel.

After the bodies of the witnesses lie dead for three and a half days, God breathes life into their bodies—and the witnesses come to their feet (Revelation 11:11). Everyone watching around the world is struck with terror. God calls the witnesses to heaven, and they ascend in a cloud—then an earthquake destroys a tenth of the city, killing seven thousand people (v. 13).

The terrified survivors, John says, give glory to God. They have experienced shock and awe. They know whose power raised the witnesses from the dead and shook the city with a mighty earthquake. They are still unrepentant—but in their terror, they give glory to God in an attempt to appease Him.

ONE ANTICHRIST, MANY ANTICHRISTS

During the Great Tribulation, Jesus will open the scroll with the seven seals, and the world will be wracked by cataclysm after cataclysm. The Antichrist will rule the world along with the False Prophet. As we have seen, it appears that Satan is preparing the

Muslim world to welcome the Antichrist as their Mahdi, and the False Prophet as Isa.

But Western civilization is not safe from the delusion of the end times. Here in America and across the Western world, our civilization is also being prepared by Satan to receive the false messiah, the Antichrist. If we don't want to be deceived when the Antichrist comes on the scene, then we must be ready—and we must be aware of the deceptive spiritual forces in our culture that would enslave us.

In our fascination with end-times prophecy, we tend to forget that the spirit of the Antichrist is already among us. The Antichrist with a capital *A* is yet to be revealed, but antichrists with a small *a* are all around us, spreading false teaching in our culture and in the church. As the apostle John wrote, "Dear children, this is the last hour; and as you have heard that the antichrist is coming, even now many antichrists have come. This is how we know it is the last hour" (1 John 2:18).

Who are these antichrists? John writes, "Who is the liar? It is whoever denies that Jesus is the Christ. Such a person is the antichrist—denying the Father and the Son" (1 John 2:22). What does it mean to deny that Jesus is the Christ?

Anyone who teaches that Jesus is one of many ways to God is an antichrist with a small *a*. Anyone who denies Jesus' claim to be the only way to God the Father is an antichrist with a small *a*. Anyone who says that Buddha or the Mahdi or Krishna is just another name for Jesus is an antichrist with a small *a*.

I believe Satan is infecting many churches today with false

teachings in order to prepare the way for the Antichrist. When the Antichrist comes, he will be hard to recognize as the Antichrist. He will be attractive and charming, and even Christians may be fooled. Jesus said that "false messiahs" will come, performing "great signs and wonders to deceive, if possible, even the elect" (Matthew 24:24).

No matter how many people the Antichrist deceives, he is ultimately destined to fall. He is the man Paul calls "the man of lawlessness" and "the man doomed to destruction" (2 Thessalonians 2:3). The prophet Daniel says that this man will rule "until the end that is decreed is poured out on him" (Daniel 9:27).

Through thousands of years of human history, human sin, and human rebellion, God has been patient. He has withheld His judgment and wrath, in spite of being blasphemed and rejected by the wicked human race. God's people have been persecuted and killed by the ungodly—and through it all, God has been patient. In fact, He has been so patient that His followers have often asked, "Lord, where are You? How much longer will You wait?"

For now, God patiently entreats people to repent and to receive His Son, Jesus. When I consider God's patience toward the human race, I think of the people I am witnessing to now who are not responding. I think of the people I have pleaded with over the years.

Many of them have locked the doors of their hearts. They always have their reasons. "Someday, maybe, I'll surrender to Christ—but I'm not ready now." "I live a good life. I don't need a Savior." "If I become a Christian, my friends will reject me." "I want to control my own life. I don't want God to tell me what to do." So many excuses—but when these people pass into eternity, what good will their excuses do for them?

When the day of wrath comes, there will be no escape, no second chances. Today, the window of salvation is still open—but for how long? The apostle Peter wrote, "The Lord is not slow in keeping his promise, as some understand slowness. Instead he is patient with you, not wanting anyone to perish, but everyone to come to repentance" (2 Peter 3:9). It is not God's will that you perish for all eternity, but God's will is not the only factor in this equation. *Your* will is also a factor. It is God's loving and gracious will that you receive the gift of eternal life—that's why He sent His Son to die for you. But God will not overrule your free will.

A day is coming when God's patience will come to an end. Let no one assume that He will tolerate sin and rebellion forever. When the Day of Judgment arrives, events will move very swiftly.

THE BOWLS OF GOD'S WRATH

In Revelation 15, John gives us a glimpse into heaven, where we see seven angels with the seven last plagues of God's wrath. The temple of heaven is filled with smoke, signifying the glory and power of God as He prepares to pour out His wrath upon a rebellious earth (v. 8).

The imagery in Revelation 15 and 16 echoes the book of Exodus. In Exodus 15:1–18, after God parted the Red Sea and His people walked between the walls of water and crossed to the other side, the Israelites sang a song of praise, called "The Song of Moses." In Revelation 15, the believers who reach heaven, who have been delivered from the oppression of Satan, will also sing a song of praise:

> Great and marvelous are your deeds,
>> Lord God Almighty.
> Just and true are your ways,
>> King of the nations.
> Who will not fear you, Lord,
>> and bring glory to your name?
> For you alone are holy.
> All nations will come
>> and worship before you,
> for your righteous acts have been revealed. (vv. 3–4)

In Exodus, Pharaoh is much more than an Egyptian king who oppressed the people of Israel. He is a symbolic type of Satan. Pharaoh's oppression of Israel symbolizes Satan's oppression of God's people today. Pharaoh was a slave driver and a tyrant, just as Satan is a slave driver and a tyrant on a global scale. Just as God delivered Israel from the clutches of Pharaoh, He will deliver us from the clutches of Satan. When that day comes, God's people will continually praise their Lord and Deliverer.

This song of praise in Revelation 15:3–4 lists five attributes of the Lord Jesus. First, He is the Creator—"Great and marvelous are your deeds." Second, He is the trustworthy Judge—"Just and true are your ways." Third, He alone is worthy of worship—"Who will not fear you, Lord, and bring glory to your name?" Fourth, He is the Holy One—"For you alone are holy." Fifth, He is Lord over all the nations—"All nations will come and worship before you."

After this song, the temple of heaven opens and seven angels come forward with seven plagues contained in seven golden bowls of judgment (Revelation 15:6–7). God is present in a special way when smoke pours from the temple. The people saw the smoke of God's presence when Solomon dedicated the first temple (2 Chronicles 7:1–3), when the prophet Isaiah saw the Lord on His throne (Isaiah 6:1–4), and when Moses ascended Mount Sinai and met God on the mountaintop (Exodus 19:18).

In Revelation 16, we see the pace of God's judgment quickening. We have become so accustomed to the patience of God that we have taken His patience for granted. As Paul writes, "Do not be deceived: God cannot be mocked. A man reaps what he sows" (Galatians 6:7). What the human race has sown by rejecting His Son is now being reaped planet-wide. In rapid succession, the seven angels go forth to pour out God's wrath upon those who have rejected Him.

In Revelation 16:1–2, the first angel pours out the first bowl of wrath, and painful sores break out on all who bear the mark of the beast and who have worshipped the image of the Antichrist. This plague of sores is a global form of the plague of boils that God inflicted on Egypt in Exodus 9:8–12.

The second angel pours his bowl upon the sea, causing the waters to become red like blood. Every living sea creature dies. Again, this is a global form of the plague in Exodus 7:17–18, when God turned the water of the Nile into blood.

The third angel pours his bowl on the rivers and springs, and all of the drinking water on earth turns to blood. The angel in charge of the waters explains that this is because

> they have shed the blood of your holy people and your
>   prophets,
>   and you have given them blood to drink as they
>   deserve. (Revelation 16:6).

Yet those who run to the blood of Jesus Christ that was shed on the cross will be shielded from God's wrath.

The fourth angel pours out his bowl upon the sun, causing the sun to burn more fiercely, scorching the earth. As human suffering intensifies, the people of the earth cry out. Do they beg for salvation and forgiveness? No! They curse God for their suffering.

The fifth angel pours his bowl directly onto the throne of the Antichrist. In that moment, the entire satanic empire of the Antichrist is plunged into darkness. When noonday brightness turns into midnight blackness, people panic—and they curse God all the more.

John writes, "But they refused to repent of what they had done" (Revelation 16:11). John finds it remarkable that the people of the world refuse to repent, and this tells us that God has not yet shut the door of salvation. These plagues are intended to drive people to God, yet they refuse.

The plague of darkness is a global version of the plague in Exodus 10:21–29, when God plunged all of Egypt into darkness. The physical darkness God inflicted on Egypt symbolized the spiritual darkness of this rebellious world. When God's people are removed from this world, the light of Christ will be removed as well. The people of earth will stumble in darkness, and their hearts will become even more hardened against God.

I believe that this scene of worldwide darkness and panic is the closest thing we will ever see to hell on earth. Yet even this is not hell. The reality of hell will be infinitely worse.

THE END OF THE ANTICHRIST'S REIGN

Turning to Revelation 17 and 18, we see that before God destroys the government of the Antichrist, He will destroy the false religious system that dominates the world. Where did this false religious system come from? It began in the Garden of Eden when Satan told Adam and Eve the oldest lie in the book: "You will be like God" (Genesis 3:5).

Satan still whispers this lie in our ears today. "You can pursue riches and fame and power, and you can be like God." "You don't need Jesus. You can choose any path to heaven, and you can be like God." "The Bible can mean anything you want it to mean. Quote it out of context, twist its meaning, make up your own religion. You can be like God." "Crystals and tarot cards, channeling and holistic healing, ritual magic and sorcery—all of these practices can give you the power to change your life. You will be like God."

Satan, the con artist, is still pitching that worn-out line—and it still works after all these years. People are still buying his lies while rejecting the truth of God's Word. That's the false religious system of this world, and God will destroy it—just before he destroys the Antichrist and his works.

As Revelation 17 opens, one of the angels of judgment says to John, "Come, I will show you the punishment of the great prostitute, who sits by many waters. With her the kings of the earth committed adultery, and the inhabitants of the earth were intoxicated with the wine of her adulteries" (vv. 1–2). Then the angel carries John in the spirit into a wilderness. There the angel shows John a woman sitting on a scarlet beast—a beast covered with blasphemous names, with seven heads and ten horns. The scarlet beast is the Antichrist; his description matches that of the Beast in Revelation 12.

The Antichrist is Satan in human form. The prostitute is dressed in purple and scarlet, with jewelry of glittering gold and precious stones. Revelation 17:5 says that across her forehead is written:

BABYLON THE GREAT

THE MOTHER OF PROSTITUTES

AND OF THE ABOMINATIONS OF THE EARTH.

In her hand, the prostitute holds a golden cup filled with sin and abomination. The woman is drunk—not with wine, but with the blood of Christian martyrs. I believe there's a deliberate symbolic parallel here. In Revelation 5, there's an interesting detail: "the four living creatures and the twenty-four elders fell down before the Lamb. Each one had a harp and they were holding golden bowls full of incense, which are the prayers of God's people" (v. 8).

Have you ever heard the saying, "God keeps our prayers in

golden bowls"? That expression comes from Revelation 5:8. The angels and elders hold golden bowls from which rise clouds of incense, the sweet-smelling prayers of God's people. It's a blessing to realize that God not only hears our prayers, but He keeps our prayers in golden bowls.

The prostitute, the woman who rides the Beast, holds a golden cup in her hand, and the cup is filled with sin and abomination, with murder and persecution. Her golden cup of sin is a mockery of the golden bowl of the prayers of God's saints.

The woman has the word "Babylon" written across her forehead. What does Babylon mean in the Bible? Babylon represents the false belief system of this world. It represents all false religions that seek to supplant faith in Christ. All false religion originates with Satan and is demonic at its core.

In the Old Testament, prostitution is often used as a symbol for a false belief system. When you see the word *idolatry* in the Bible, it is often used synonymously with *adultery* or *prostitution*. Both idolatry and adultery involve unfaithfulness. An adulterous husband is unfaithful to his wife. An adulterous wife is unfaithful to her husband. And those who practice idolatry are unfaithful to God.

In the Old Testament, God told the prophet Hosea to marry an unfaithful woman, a prostitute. Hosea married her, yet she soon went back to prostitution. Brokenhearted, Hosea still loved her and forgave her. By forgiving and accepting his wife after she was unfaithful to him, Hosea demonstrated God's love for the unfaithful people of Israel.

In the closing verses of Revelation 17, we see the destruction of the prostitute of Revelation. The angel says to John, "The beast and the ten horns you saw will hate the prostitute. They will bring her to ruin and leave her naked; they will eat her flesh and burn her with fire" (Revelation 17:16).

At first the prostitute, the false religious system, comes riding on the back of the Antichrist. She even appears to control the Antichrist. But in the end, the Antichrist turns on the false religious system and destroys it. Why does the Antichrist destroy his ally, the false religious system?

Answer: the Antichrist views the false religious system not as an ally but as a competitor. The Antichrist wants the whole world to worship him alone. His alliance with the false religious system will last as long as it benefits them. And when the prostitute outlives her usefulness, the Beast will destroy her without a second thought.

The false religious system is not some future religion that will arise in the end times. This false religion is with us today. It pervades every corner of our culture and has infected the church. One of the doctrines of this false system is a notion called universalism. It's the idea that it doesn't matter what you believe, as long as you are sincere; there are many paths to God, and a loving God wouldn't turn anyone away. That's the prostitute of Revelation 17.

This false notion will gain global acceptance and deceive the masses. The Antichrist will permit this false belief system to go on for a while as he gains power. But a point will come when this false religion no longer serves his purposes—and that point occurs halfway through the Tribulation. That's when the False Prophet sets up the image of the Antichrist in the temple and forces the world to worship the Antichrist or be killed.

At the moment the Antichrist demands the worship of the world, universalism is no longer his ally—it's his enemy. He will demand to be worshipped as a god. He can tolerate no other God. The Antichrist will be Satan's imitation-Christ—that's why he's the Anti-Christ, the opposite of Christ. Paul describes the Antichrist this way:

> Don't let anyone deceive you in any way, for that day will not come until the rebellion occurs and the man of lawlessness is revealed, the man doomed to destruction. He will oppose and will exalt himself over everything that is called God or is worshiped, so that he sets himself up in God's temple, proclaiming himself to be God. (2 Thessalonians 2:3–4)

When the Antichrist declares himself to be God, those who claim there are many paths to God will become enemies of the Antichrist. The totalitarian religion of the Antichrist will permit no dissent. The Antichrist's reign will be global, so there will be no place to hide, no place beyond his reach.

Don't be misled by talk of peace and global harmony. Don't be misled by talk of higher consciousness or mantras or spiritual healing. There's nothing new about so-called New Age practices. Those beliefs and rituals were practiced in ancient Babylon, thousands of years ago. That's why the book of Revelation uses Babylon as a symbol of false religion. There is nothing new under the sun.

In Revelation 19, we encounter a scene where John hears a great multitude in heaven, shouting:

Hallelujah!
Salvation and glory and power belong to our God,
    for true and just are his judgments.
He has condemned the great prostitute
    who corrupted the earth by her adulteries.
He has avenged on her the blood of his servants. (vv. 1–2)

This song says that *God* condemned the great prostitute. Yet Revelation 17:16 says the Antichrist and his allies destroyed the prostitute, the false religious system: "They will bring her to ruin and leave her naked; they will eat her flesh and burn her with fire." If it was the Antichrist who destroyed the prostitute, then why does the heavenly multitude praise God for her destruction?

This is an important lesson regarding the sovereignty of God. This passage shows that even the treachery of the Antichrist serves God's purpose. The Antichrist had a selfish motive for destroying the false religious system. The Antichrist wanted to be worshipped as God, so he eliminated all competition.

But the Antichrist's treachery served to avenge the blood of God's martyrs. When the Antichrist destroyed the false religious system, the multitude in heaven shouted, "Hallelujah! / The smoke from her goes up for ever and ever" (Revelation 19:3).

The symbolic Babylon, the great prostitute, has been destroyed by fire. Evil has destroyed evil, God is glorified, and heaven resounds with praise: "Hallelujah! / For our Lord God Almighty reigns!" (v. 6).

SATAN'S ONE GREAT FEAR

On December 5, 1996, Federal Reserve Board Chairman Alan Greenspan gave a rather technical speech about the economy at the American Enterprise Institute. No one expected any shockwaves from the speech, least of all Greenspan himself. At one point, Greenspan asked, "How do we know when irrational exuberance has unduly escalated asset values?" That kind of rhetoric puts most people to sleep—but professional investors heard those words and *panicked.*

The Tokyo stock market was open while Greenspan was speaking, and by the time the market closed, news of Greenspan's speech had shaken Japanese investors like an earthquake. Stock prices plunged. As other markets opened around the world, the sell-offs continued. The stock market lost billions of dollars of value in a day.

Why? Two words: *irrational exuberance.* Without meaning to, Greenspan had set off a stampede of selling. Investors misinterpreted his words, and a jittery global market overreacted. The moral of this story is that it wouldn't take much to send the global economy into a full-blown meltdown. If two words could send waves of panic around the world in 1996, imagine how today's markets would react to a Middle East war or a debt default by a major industrial nation.

Revelation 18 depicts the destruction of the global economic system and global political system of the Antichrist. All who place their confidence in wealth will despair when the economic system crashes. The wealthiest people in the world will lose everything in a single day. Only those who invest in heavenly futures will have true net worth.

The chronology of these events is unclear. Many of the events depicted in Revelation 18 and 19 seem to occur at the same time as the signs of judgment elsewhere in Revelation. For example, Revelation 6:1–8 depicts the opening of the first four seals of God's judgment. Each seal is represented by a rider on horseback. These riders unleash a series of calamities. The rider on the black horse brings economic devastation, famine, and death. So Revelation 18 and Revelation 6:1–8 seem to describe the same global economic collapse.

In the final days of the Great Tribulation, the Antichrist will see his global empire collapsing to ruin all around him. He has had seven years to reign over the earth; seven years to receive the worship of the masses; seven years to rule the world. And in the final days of his empire, the Antichrist will realize that his doom is approaching.

In the time he has left, the Antichrist will unleash as much destruction as he can. We tend to think of Satan as a powerful and terrifying creature, and he is. But in that day, it will be the Antichrist, Satan in human form, who will be terrified. The devil has one great fear: he fears the final judgment. That's why he hates to be reminded of it.

In the next chapter, we will see the Antichrist gather his forces for his last stand—the Battle of Armageddon.

PART 3

THE WAR
TO END ALL WARS

Is the End Closer Than We Think?

FIVE

SLOUCHING TOWARD ARMAGEDDON

FRENCH CHEMIST Pierre Eugène Marcellin Berthelot (1827–1907) was one of the great prophets of science. He had an uncanny ability to look at the state of scientific knowledge in his own time, then project that knowledge far into the future and make accurate predictions. He believed that science could bring about a utopia by the year 2000, but he also worried that scientific knowledge might destroy the human race.

He once wrote, "Within a hundred years . . . men will know what the atom is. It is my belief when science reaches this stage, God will come down to earth with His big ring of keys and will say to humanity, 'Gentlemen, it is closing time.'"[1]

Those are prophetic words indeed. Less than a hundred years after Marcellin Berthelot wrote those words, atomic bombs were dropped on two Japanese cities, ending World War II. Since then, the human race has lived in fear of nuclear annihilation, waiting for "closing time."

That day is coming. It will arrive at the end of a turbulent seven-year period known as the Great Tribulation. On that day, the most violent and decisive battle in the history of the world will take place—a conflict known as the Battle of Armageddon. You may think you know what the Battle of Armageddon will be and where it will be fought, but as we delve deeply into the book of Revelation, you may be surprised.

The word "Armageddon" appears only once in the entire Bible, in Revelation 16:16: "Then they gathered the kings together to the place that in Hebrew is called Armageddon." Though this verse does not contain a lot of information, there is much that we can and should know about this future battle.

In 1920, the Irish poet William Butler Yeats published a poem called "The Second Coming," in which he described a "blood-dimmed tide" sweeping over the world. "Surely some revelation is at hand," he warned, then he concluded:

Twenty centuries of stony sleep
Were vexed to nightmare by a rocking cradle,
And what rough beast, its hour come round at last,
Slouches towards Bethlehem to be born?[2]

Yeats envisions a Beast—the Antichrist—arriving on the scene at the appointed hour, ominous and dreadful, slouching toward Bethlehem to be born. Yeats was a poet, not a theologian. There's nothing in Scripture to suggest that the Antichrist will be born in Bethlehem as Christ was.

But we have God's Word on this: the "rough beast" known

as the Antichrist will one day slouch toward Armageddon to be defeated.

A scene in Revelation 10 tells us a lot about the final days of human history. This scene takes place during an intermission between the sixth and seventh trumpet judgments. As Revelation 10 opens, we meet a mighty angel on a sacred mission. This angel comes wrapped in a cloud, which speaks of the presence and power of God. The angel also has a rainbow over his head, symbolizing God's faithfulness to His promises. The angel's face shines like the sun, because he has been in the presence of God. He stands with his right foot upon the sea and his left foot upon the land, symbolizing his God-given authority over the earth.

In the palm of his hand the angel holds a small, open scroll. A voice like seven thunders speaks to John. Seven, as we have seen, is the number of perfection and completion, which tells us that this is the voice of God. The Lord gives John a message and tells him to seal the message, to keep it hidden. Then God gives John another message: "Go, take the scroll that lies open in the hand of the angel who is standing on the sea and on the land" (Revelation 10:8).

John takes the scroll and the angel says, "Take it and eat it. It will turn your stomach sour, but 'in your mouth it will be as sweet as honey'" (Revelation 10:9).

This little scroll is about to reveal the mystery of God and the mystery of human life on earth. John takes the scroll and eats it. Just as the angel promised, the scroll tastes sweet in John's mouth, but it turns to bitterness in his stomach.

What does this mean? When the Bible speaks of "eating" a book, it doesn't mean consuming the paper. It means internalizing the message written on its pages. To those who love God, the Word of God is sweet to the taste. The Psalmist tells us, "How sweet are your words to my taste, / sweeter than honey to my mouth!" (Psalm 119:103).

This scene in Revelation parallels a scene in the book of Ezekiel—but with an important difference. When God commissioned Ezekiel to be His prophet to Israel, God told him, "Eat this scroll; then go and speak to the people of Israel" (Ezekiel 3:1). So Ezekiel ate the scroll and it was as sweet in his mouth as honey. But unlike John, Ezekiel found that the scroll was also sweet to his stomach—he didn't experience the bitterness and upset stomach that John felt. Why?

The scroll God gave Ezekiel contained a message of judgment and destruction, but it was also a message that the judgment would come to an end after seventy years of exile. The people of Israel would return to their homeland to rebuild the temple and the city of Jerusalem, and the nation would be blessed. So the Word of God, which is always sweet in the mouth, was also sweet in Ezekiel's stomach because it was ultimately a message of hope.

But the message God gave to John was a message of judgment and destruction—and those whom God was about to judge would have no hope. They would never rebuild. They would never be blessed. So the Word of God was sweet in John's mouth, but it was bitter in his stomach because it was a message of unrelenting doom for everyone whose sins are not covered by the blood of Christ.

THE KINGS FROM THE EAST

While moving through the Great Tribulation, we have seen a series of cataclysms in groups of sevens—seven seals, seven trumpets, and seven bowls of judgment. We have seen earthquakes, an eclipse of the sun, the moon turning to blood, the stars falling from the heavens, and the mountains and islands shaken out of their places.

In Revelation 16, we see the seven bowls of God's wrath—a series of plagues much like the plagues God inflicted on Egypt in Moses' day, only on a global scale. The first bowl is a plague of painful sores. The second bowl turns the sea into blood. The third bowl turns the rivers to blood. The fourth bowl causes the sun to blaze hotter. The fifth bowl plunges the world into darkness.

Now we come to the sixth bowl of God's wrath, described in Revelation 16:12. The sixth angel pours out his bowl upon the Euphrates River. The river dries up, opening a clear path for an invasion by "the kings from the East." What does it mean for the Euphrates to dry up? It means that conditions are ripe for satanic forces to be unleashed and for the Battle of Armageddon to begin.

The Euphrates is a natural boundary established by God. It has its source in eastern Turkey, flows through Syria and Iraq, then joins the Tigris and empties into the Persian Gulf. In ancient times, the Euphrates formed the western boundary of the Persian Empire. By drying up the river, God erases that natural boundary and unleashes evil forces on the world—forces called "the kings of the East."

Who are these kings of the East? They are not human beings. As we compare scripture with scripture, it becomes clear that these kings are demonic rulers. The Bible tells us that invisible kings and princes have been assigned to nations and empires on the earth. These forces are part of the spiritual hierarchy of Satan's kingdom. In Deuteronomy 4:19, God warns Israel not to worship spirits on the earth or in the sky: "Do not be enticed into bowing down to them and worshiping things the LORD your God has apportioned to all the nations under heaven."

There is another reference in Deuteronomy to God dividing the nations among angelic or demonic beings—but the meaning of that verse is obscured in the New International Version. It reads:

> When the Most High gave the nations their inheritance,
>   when he divided all mankind,
> he set up boundaries for the peoples
>   according to the number of the sons of Israel.
> (Deuteronomy 32:8)

That phrase "the sons of Israel" comes from the Masoretic Hebrew text. But the ancient text of the Dead Sea Scrolls reads differently; instead of "the sons of Israel," it reads "the sons of God." In Genesis and Job, the term "sons of God" refers to both fallen and unfallen angels. The Greek Septuagint reads "the angels of God." Many Bible translators have chosen to follow the Dead Sea Scrolls and Septuagint sense: "He assigned to each nation a heavenly being" (Good News Translation), "divine beings" (New American Bible, Revised Edition), and "the heavenly assembly" (New English Translation).

It is clear that "the sons of God" or "the angels of God" is the correct sense of that verse, because the next verse reads:

For the LORD's portion is his people,
Jacob his allotted inheritance. (Deuteronomy 32:9)

In other words, Moses is saying in these two verses that when God divided up the nations and set boundaries for the people, He assigned "the sons of God," the heavenly assembly of angels, to the various nations and kingdoms—all except the nation of Israel. The Lord assigned Himself to be the spiritual ruler of Jacob's nation, Israel. All other nations are spiritually ruled by an angelic "prince" or "king." As you study everything the Scriptures have to say about these spiritual rulers of nations, it seems clear that they are fallen angels—demons—under the command of Satan.

The prophet Isaiah also refers to these invisible powers and kings:

In that day the LORD will punish
the powers in the heavens above
and the kings on the earth below. (Isaiah 24:21)

In Ephesians 6:12, the apostle Paul speaks of our spiritual struggle "against the rulers, against the authorities, against the powers of this dark world." In Colossians 1:16, he speaks of "things in heaven and on earth, visible and invisible, whether thrones or powers or rulers or authorities."

The most profound and detailed reference to these demonic spiritual rulers is found in the book of Daniel. In Daniel 10:13, we read of the demonic prince of Persia, who detained God's messenger and could only be overcome with the help of the archangel Michael. And in Daniel 10:20, the messenger refers to the prince of Greece—the demonic being who rules over that nation. In Psalm 82, we read of God's judgment against these invisible kings (the Psalmist calls them "gods"):

> God presides in the great assembly;
>> he renders judgment among the "gods" . . .
>
> "The 'gods' know nothing, they understand nothing.
>> They walk about in darkness;
>> all the foundations of the earth are shaken.
>
> "I said, 'You are "gods";
>> you are all sons of the Most High.'
> But you will die like mere mortals;
>> you will fall like every other ruler."
>
> Rise up, O God, judge the earth,
>> for all the nations are your inheritance.
>
> (Psalm 82:1, 5–8)

America has spent decades, thousands of American lives, and trillions of dollars trying to bring order and stability to the Persian Gulf region. Who dominates the Persian Gulf? Iran—the nation the Bible calls Persia. Through its many client states—Lebanon, Syria, Iraq, Yemen—the Persian nation of Iran dominates the region.

In 2015, leaders of the United States and other countries forged an agreement with Iran to prevent that nation from acquiring nuclear weapons. Our leaders and negotiators had no idea who or what they were negotiating with. I'm certain that, sitting across the table from them, was an invisible presence—the same presence that struggled with the messenger to Daniel and the archangel Michael—the demonic prince of Persia. After all these centuries, the invisible ruler of Persia is still calling the shots in that land.

God has chosen not to tell us very much about these invisible kings. He has told us just enough that we would be aware of them, but not so much that we would become obsessed with them. God doesn't want us to be mesmerized by the kingdom of darkness. He wants us to keep our eyes fixed on Him.

THE ARMY OF TWO HUNDRED MILLION

As we have seen, Revelation is written as a series of themes, not a chronological narrative. For example, there is a section in Revelation 9 that relates to these events in Revelation 16. In Revelation 9:14, God tells the angel with the sixth trumpet, "Release the four angels who are bound at the great river Euphrates." John goes on to say, "The four angels who had been kept ready for this very hour and day and month and year were released to kill a third of mankind." I believe the release of the four angels in Revelation 9 and the drying of the Euphrates in Revelation 16 are the same event.

In Revelation 9:16, John makes an intriguing statement: "The number of the mounted troops was twice ten thousand times ten thousand. I heard their number." Now, I have to admit that I flunked math in school. I'm not joking; I really did. But I can use a calculator, and I worked out what "twice ten thousand times ten thousand" means: two hundred million. To put it in numerical form, John is talking about 200,000,000 soldiers.

That is a shocking number. In fact John himself finds it incomprehensible. That's why he says at the end of that verse, "I heard their number" (Revelation 9:16). He's saying, in effect, "I know! I can hardly believe it myself! But that's the number I heard."

No nation on earth has a standing army of two hundred million soldiers. In fact, when John wrote this prophecy, the population of the entire world didn't equal two hundred million people. Today, the largest army in the world belongs to the People's Republic of China—about two million soldiers. That's 1 percent of the army John describes here.

I believe there can only be one explanation: the two hundred million soldiers John speaks of can only be demonic forces.

There's another important symbol regarding the Euphrates. As you know, the Garden of Eden was located by the Euphrates; so was the Tower of Babel. The Euphrates region was the cradle of civilization, and it will be the grave of civilization. In Revelation 16, John describes what he saw immediately after the angel dried up the Euphrates River:

> Then I saw three impure spirits that looked like frogs; they
> came out of the mouth of the dragon, out of the mouth of

the beast and out of the mouth of the false prophet. They are demonic spirits that perform signs, and they go out to the kings of the whole world, to gather them for the battle on the great day of God Almighty. (vv. 13–14)

Three unclean spirits proceed from the mouths of Satan, the Antichrist, and the False Prophet—the "unholy trinity" of the end times. Impure or unclean spirits are demons, and frogs are a symbol of uncleanness. In Persia, frogs were thought to carry plagues. Among the Jews, frogs were seen as messengers of Satan. These froglike demons go forth to deceive humanity, and they will fight in the Battle of Armageddon.

There is a significant intermission between the sixth and seventh bowls of God's judgment in Revelation 16. There, the Lord inserts a parenthetical statement—and it's a powerful one. He says:

Look, I come like a thief! Blessed is the one who stays awake and remains clothed, so as not to go naked and be shamefully exposed. (v. 15)

I have heard this verse quoted as a warning to be ready for the Lord's return. But I think the Lord gave it to us as a message of encouragement. This verse always blesses me. It tells me that even though the world is plunging headlong into depravity, we can trust God. Don't lose heart; don't lose faith. The Lord will come like a thief, when the world least expects Him.

If the words "I come like a thief" sound familiar, it's because Jesus made a similar statement to His disciples:

Therefore keep watch, because you do not know on what day your Lord will come. But understand this: If the owner of the house had known at what time of night the thief was coming, he would have kept watch and would not have let his house be broken into. So you also must be ready, because the Son of Man will come at an hour when you do not expect him. (Matthew 24:42–44)

The apostle Paul used that same metaphor: "You know very well that the day of the Lord will come like a thief in the night" (1 Thessalonians 5:2). And the apostle Peter used it as well: "The day of the Lord will come like a thief. The heavens will disappear with a roar; the elements will be destroyed by fire, and the earth and everything done in it will be laid bare" (2 Peter 3:10). We should heed every word God tells us—but when He makes the same statement *four times* in His Word, we *really* need to take notice.

The Day of the Lord will come like a thief to those who are spiritually asleep, but we who are alert and watchful know it's going to be a great day.

A GLIMPSE OF THE SECOND COMING

The original Greek New Testament refers to the Second Coming as the *parousia* ("coming" or "arrival") of Christ. The early church's view of the Second Coming is summed up with dignity and simplicity in the Nicene Creed: "He will come again in glory to judge the living and the dead and his kingdom will have no end."[3]

Down through the centuries, different views of the Second Coming have emerged. One of the best-known interpretations of the Second Coming is the "dispensationalist" view that was popularized by the *Scofield Reference Bible*, the 1970s bestseller *The Late, Great Planet Earth*, and the popular Left Behind series of novels. According to this view, Jesus will return to earth not once, but twice. These two events are known as the Rapture (from the Latin *raptus*, meaning "a carrying off") and the Second Coming. Although this is the most widely known view of the Second Coming among American evangelicals, it was completely unknown until the 1800s, and it is not the traditionally held Protestant view.

I want to be clear in stating that I hold to an evangelical, Reformed view, and I believe there are major problems with the more widely popularized view—but that doesn't mean that those who hold other views of the Second Coming are heretical or unsaved. Our salvation does not depend on any particular doctrine of the Second Coming.

The popular view, the Left Behind view, is that there will be a "secret Rapture" in which all genuine Christians vanish from the world and meet Jesus in the air, and all unbelievers are left behind to go through the Great Tribulation. The "secret Rapture" notion is based on what I believe to be a misunderstanding of the Lord's words in the Olivet Discourse (His description of the end times in Matthew 24, Mark 13, and Luke 21): "Two men will be in the field; one will be taken and the other left" (Matthew 24:40). These words describe the Rapture, when the Lord returns to take His church out of the world. But there's nothing in the Lord's words to suggest that the Rapture will be secret—only that it will be sudden and unexpected.

When you compare scripture with scripture, it is clear that the

Rapture will be a loud and startling event. The arrival of Jesus for His church will be instantly known to the entire world. In fact, the evidence indicates that the Rapture and the Second Coming are not two events but the same event. The apostle Paul's account of the Rapture/Second Coming is a vivid description of a very loud event, accompanied by a shout and a trumpet call:

> For we believe that Jesus died and rose again, and so we believe that God will bring with Jesus those who have fallen asleep in him. According to the Lord's word, we tell you that we who are still alive, who are left until the coming of the Lord, will certainly not precede those who have fallen asleep. For the Lord himself will come down from heaven, with a loud command, with the voice of the archangel and with the trumpet call of God, and the dead in Christ will rise first. After that, we who are still alive and are left will be caught up together with them in the clouds to meet the Lord in the air. And so we will be with the Lord forever. (1 Thessalonians 4:14–17)

This is consistent with the way Jesus Himself described the Second Coming in the Olivet Discourse (notice again the trumpet call):

> Then will appear the sign of the Son of Man in heaven. And then all the peoples of the earth will mourn when they see the Son of Man coming on the clouds of heaven, with power and great glory. And he will send his angels

with a loud trumpet call, and they will gather his elect from the four winds, from one end of the heavens to the other. (Matthew 24:30–31)

Jesus says that, when He gathers His followers, all the people of the earth will see Him. They will mourn because they have rejected Him, just as John writes in Revelation 1:7:

"Look, he is coming with the clouds,"
    and "every eye will see him,
even those who pierced him";
    and all peoples on earth "will mourn because of him."

So I believe that the Rapture and the Second Coming of Christ are the same event. It will be the most widely viewed event in the history of the human race.

If you hold to a different view, then God bless you, we can still be brothers and sisters in the Lord and one in the Spirit. Our views on the Second Coming of Christ must not divide us. What matters is that we believe that Jesus is Lord, He died for our sins, He rose again, He shall come again in glory to judge the living and the dead, and His kingdom shall have no end.

THE LAST GOSPEL MESSAGE

In Revelation 14:6–12, three angels make a series of pronouncements. The first angel flies overhead and proclaims "the eternal gospel" (v. 6). This message goes out to every human being on earth, to every nation, in every language: "Fear God and give him glory, because the hour of his judgment has come. Worship him who made the heavens, the earth, the sea and the springs of water" (v. 7).

The door of salvation is still open, but it won't be for long. This is the last time the gospel will ever be offered to the human race before judgment and destruction fall. In the darkest period of human history, the light of the gospel breaks through. Even now, God is not willing that any should perish. This is the only place in Revelation where the word "gospel" appears, and it is the last time the gospel is mentioned in the Bible.

Next, the second angel announces, "'Fallen! Fallen is Babylon the Great,' which made all the nations drink the maddening wine of her adulteries" (Revelation 14:8). But the fall of Babylon has not yet taken place in Revelation. That will occur in Revelation 18; the entire chapter is devoted to God's judgment against Babylon. Like so many symbols and events in Revelation, the fall of Babylon is not depicted on a chronological timetable. Instead, Babylon's fall is a recurring theme throughout Revelation. God is not subject to time as we are. In His presence, all of time—past, present, and future—exist as one.

Some people believe that the "Babylon" in the book of Revelation is the literal city of Babylon, which lies in ruins in Iraq today, about fifty miles south of Baghdad. Many prophecy-minded Christians became very excited in the 1980s when Saddam Hussein spent billions of dollars to restore ancient Babylon to its former glory. They said, "You see? The city of Babylon is going to be central to the end times." But the rebuilding of Babylon ended when

Saddam Hussein's regime was toppled by American-led forces in 2003. Today, the site of ancient Babylon is still a field of ruins.

I believe Babylon is a symbol of any culture or nation that sets itself against the will of God. In the context of Revelation, Babylon seems to represent the combined political-religious system of the Antichrist and the False Prophet. Whether this "Babylon" is literal or symbolic is a minor matter. We should always major on the majors, not the minors.

Next, the third angel proclaims:

> If anyone worships the beast and its image and receives its mark on their forehead or on their hand, they, too, will drink the wine of God's fury, which has been poured full strength into the cup of his wrath. They will be tormented with burning sulfur in the presence of the holy angels and of the Lamb. And the smoke of their torment will rise for ever and ever. There will be no rest day or night for those who worship the beast and its image, or for anyone who receives the mark of its name. (Revelation 14:9–11)

All who worship the Beast will drink the undiluted wine of God's wrath. There will be no mercy mixed into the cup of God's anger. There will be no more opportunities for salvation.

After these pronouncements comes a blessing from heaven:

> Then I heard a voice from heaven say, "Write this: Blessed are the dead who die in the Lord from now on."

"Yes," says the Spirit, "they will rest from their labor, for their deeds will follow them." (Revelation 14:13)

I have often heard these words quoted at funerals, and I think it's valid to use this verse to comfort those who grieve. In context, this verse speaks to the tremendous suffering of those Last Days. Yet embedded in this verse is an encouraging insight. Even in these final moments of the Great Tribulation, just before the gavel of God's justice crashes down upon the earth, some people respond to the gospel—and they will be saved. They will suffer tremendous persecution. The forces of the Antichrist will hunt them down and death will be a tremendous blessing. The horrors of the Tribulation will make death seem like blessed rest.

Believers who remain loyal to the Lord Jesus will be blessed indeed. Jesus said, "Blessed are you when people insult you, persecute you and falsely say all kinds of evil against you because of me" (Matthew 5:11). Patient endurance through persecution brings God's blessing to our lives.

ARMAGEDDON AND THE GRAPES OF GOD'S WRATH

In the closing verses of Revelation 14, we see that the hour for reaping has come. John sees a white cloud, and seated on the cloud is the Son of Man. He wears a golden crown. In His hand is a sickle. An angel from the heavenly temple shouts, "Take your sickle and reap, because the time to reap has come, for the harvest of the earth is ripe" (v. 15). So the Son of Man—the Judge of the earth—swings His sickle and harvests the earth. The grapes are thrown into the winepress of God's wrath.

That winepress has a name: Armageddon.

Here again, we see that the images and themes of Revelation are not presented to us in chronological order. The winepress and the crushing of the grapes in Revelation 14 are symbols of the same event John later describes in Revelation 16 and 19—an event that is commonly known as the Battle of Armageddon.

The word *Armageddon* comes from the ancient Greek word *Harmagedōn*, which many Bible scholars trace back to the Hebrew *Har Megiddô*. The word *Har* is a shortened form of *Harar*, which means a hill or mountain. Har Megiddô is a particular kind of hill known as a *tell*—a hill created by hundreds of years of having fortresses built, destroyed, then rebuilt on the same spot. Har Megiddô, or Armageddon, is a man-made hill made up of layers and layers of ruined fortresses. It has been the site of countless battles down through the centuries.

These fortresses stood guard over the Via Maris, the ancient trade route linking Egypt, Anatolia (Asia Minor), Syria, and Mesopotamia. Various battles of Megiddo have been fought there, including a 1457 BC battle between Egyptian forces and a Canaanite coalition, a 609 BC battle between the Egyptians and the nation of Judah (2 Kings 23 and 2 Chronicles 35), and the 1918 Battle of Megiddo, when the British defeated the Ottoman Empire during World War I. The Plain of Megiddo is inland from the Israeli coastal city of Haifa and is located about fifty-five miles north of Jerusalem.

Many evangelical scholars interpret the battle scenes in Revelation as a literal military conflict fought on the Plain of Megiddo. According to this view, the armies of many nations will gather for war and the human armies will be like grapes crushed in the winepress of God's wrath. Revelation 14:20 says that "blood flowed out of the press, rising as high as the horses' bridles for a distance of 1,600 stadia." This would be a battle of unparalleled violence and bloodshed. A distance of 1,600 stadia equals about 180 miles. Israel is only 263 miles long from north to south. So John envisions a lake of blood some five feet deep, extending more than two-thirds the length of the state of Israel.

But there is another view of this final battle—a view held by many evangelical theologians. According to this view, the Greek *Harmagedōn* is actually derived from the Hebrew *Har Mo'wed*, which means "Mount of Assembly" or "Mount of the Congregation," which refers to Mount Zion. In fact, John tells us that, at the outset of this final battle, the Lord Jesus will come to earth and stand on Mount Zion (Revelation 14:1).

Does John refer to a literal geographical site called Mount Zion—or does Mount Zion symbolize a deeper spiritual reality? To answer that question, let's first examine the historical Mount Zion. According to tradition, Mount Zion is the Temple Mount—the "Mount of Assembly," where the congregation of Israel gathered to worship the Lord. Mount Zion first appears in the Bible in 2 Samuel 5:7: "Nevertheless, David captured the fortress of Zion—which is the City of David." Before King David established Jerusalem as Israel's capital, the city belonged to a Canaanite tribe, the Jebusites, and their fortress was called Zion.

If Armageddon refers to *Har Mo'wed*, the "Mount of Congregation" or Mount Zion, then what sort of battle will it be? Many evangelical theologians believe that the final battle of the book of Revelation will not involve human armies and weapons of warfare. Instead, these images of horrifying violence might be vivid symbols describing a battle in the *spiritual* realm. It would be the decisive final assault in the war Paul wrote about (Ephesians 6:12). The Battle of Armageddon is described in greater detail in Revelation 19:

I saw heaven standing open and there before me was a white horse, whose rider is called Faithful and True. With justice he judges and wages war. His eyes are like blazing fire, and on his head are many crowns. He has a name written on him that no one knows but he himself. He is dressed in a robe dipped in blood, and his name is the Word of God. The armies of heaven were following him, riding on white horses and dressed in fine linen, white and clean. Coming out of his mouth is a sharp sword with which to strike down the nations. "He will rule them with an iron scepter." He treads the winepress of the fury of the wrath of God Almighty. On his robe and on his thigh he has this name written:

KING OF KINGS AND LORD OF LORDS.

And I saw an angel standing in the sun, who cried in a loud voice to all the birds flying in midair, "Come, gather together for the great supper of God, so that you may eat the flesh of kings, generals, and the mighty, of horses and their riders, and the flesh of all people, free and slave, great and small." (vv. 11–18)

Here again, God's wrath is described as a winepress. But is this a physical battle or a spiritual battle? Is it a clash between nations and armies—or between rulers, authorities, and forces of the spiritual realm?

ARMAGEDDON IN THE OLD TESTAMENT

I lean toward the belief that the Battle of Armageddon will be a spiritual battle rather than a military conflict. And let's be clear on this: spiritual warfare is no less real, no less deadly, and no less frightening than military warfare. If anything, spiritual warfare is even *more* appalling, because eternal destinies are at stake—and Satan and his fallen angels are the cunning, ruthless foes.

In Revelation 16:12, the sixth angel pours out his bowl upon the Euphrates River, and the river goes dry, opening a path for invasion by "the kings from the East," who bring a force of two hundred million soldiers with them. As we have seen, no nation on earth could field an army of two hundred million soldiers, but it is conceivable that the demonic forces of Satan may well number two hundred million demons or more. In fact, the Battle of Armageddon would almost have to be a battle between spiritual forces, not human forces, because it would be physically impossible for such a vast number of human soldiers to fight each other in the confined space of the Plain of Megiddo.

John seems to describe *supernatural* preparations for this ultimate battle, not military preparations. Revelation 16:14 tells us that the three froglike demons that came from the mouths of the Dragon, the Beast, and the False Prophet "go out to the kings of the whole world, to gather them for the battle on the great day of God Almighty." As we have already seen, "kings of the whole world" is probably a reference to the invisible demonic rulers of the nations of the world, not a reference to human leaders of nations.

There are many prophecies of this ultimate conflict in the Old Testament, and they often make the most sense when interpreted as a spiritual battle rather than a military battle. In Isaiah 13, for example, the prophet describes how the nations gather for war and the Lord assembles a host for battle. The sun and moon go dark, the heavens are shaken, and the Lord and His host destroy their enemies. Then, in Isaiah 14, the Lord tells His people to take up a taunt against the defeated king of Babylon—and it quickly becomes clear that the king of Babylon is a symbol for Satan. Here is an excerpt:

How the oppressor has come to an end!
    How his fury has ended! . . .

How you have fallen from heaven,
    morning star, son of the dawn!
You have been cast down to the earth,
    you who once laid low the nations!
You said in your heart,
    "I will ascend to the heavens;

I will raise my throne
>above the stars of God;
I will sit enthroned on the mount of assembly,
>on the utmost heights of Mount Zaphon.
I will ascend above the tops of the clouds;
>I will make myself like the Most High."
But you are brought down to the realm of the dead,
>to the depths of the pit. (vv. 4, 12–15)

It seems likely that the Mount Zion the Scriptures speak of—the "mount of assembly" where the Lord will make His stand against the forces of Satan—is probably a symbol for the church. In the New Testament letter to the Hebrews, the term "Mount Zion" is clearly used as a metaphor for the church:

> But you have come to Mount Zion, to the city of the living God, the heavenly Jerusalem. You have come to thousands upon thousands of angels in joyful assembly, to the church of the firstborn, whose names are written in heaven. You have come to God, the Judge of all, to the spirits of the righteous made perfect. (Hebrews 12:22–23)

If we view the final battle of Revelation as a violent, all-out assault against Mount Zion (the church) by the cruel and hateful forces of Satan—a battle in the spiritual realm—then it takes on a whole new meaning. The demon forces seek to conquer Mount Zion, not the physical Temple Mount in Jerusalem but the *spiritual* Mount Zion, the church. Satan despises the church. He is beside himself with rage toward us as believers because we will inherit heaven—the paradise that Satan himself has lost. Through the church, God demonstrates His manifold wisdom to all the fallen angels and demonic rulers in the heavenly realms (Ephesians 3:10). So this ultimate battle is Satan's final attempt to destroy the followers of Christ, which the Bible identifies symbolically as "Mount Zion."

Again and again, we see this battle depicted in Old Testament prophecy as an assault against Mount Zion. Micah 4:11 reveals Satan's hatred against Zion as he gathers the demon-kings of the nations for battle: "Let her be defiled, / let our eyes gloat over Zion!" In Joel 2:1 we read, "Blow the trumpet in Zion; / sound the alarm on my holy hill. / Let all who live in the land tremble, / for the day of the Lord is coming." In Obadiah 1:15 and 17, we read, "The day of the LORD is near . . . But on Mount Zion will be deliverance." And Isaiah 31:4 tells us, ". . . the LORD Almighty will come down / to do battle on Mount Zion"—a scene that is echoed in Revelation 14:1: "Then I looked, and there before me was the Lamb, standing on Mount Zion."

And here's one of the most compelling reasons that I believe the Battle of Armageddon will be fought on a spiritual battlefield rather than the physical Plain of Megiddo: It makes absolutely no sense for Satan and his demons to gather the nations of the world to attack Jerusalem. The Antichrist already controls the *physical* city of Jerusalem; it's the capital of his global empire. But it makes perfect sense for Satan and his demons to wage an all-out assault against the *spiritual* Mount Zion, the church.

One day, after these prophecies have been fulfilled, we will know for sure whether this was the bloodiest military conflict in human history—or the decisive final battle in the heavenly realms. Even if you and I disagree over the interpretation of these prophecies, we agree that Jesus is Lord and that He will win the battle. On that foundation of truth, we are blessedly united.

I should make one final observation. I have been referring to this ultimate battle by the name most commonly used: the Battle of Armageddon. The Scriptures, however, never refer to the battle by that name. In the Old Testament, it is usually called "the Day of the Lord." In Revelation 16:14, John calls it "the battle on the great day of God Almighty." For those faithful believers who love Jesus, it will truly be the great day of God Almighty. If you belong to the Lord Jesus, you have nothing to fear from this battle. In fact, you can look forward with joy and expectation to the great day of God Almighty.

IT MEANS GOD WINS

Next, John reveals the ultimate fate of two members of the unholy trinity—the Antichrist and the False Prophet:

> Then I saw the beast and the kings of the earth and their armies gathered together to wage war against the rider on the horse and his army. But the beast was captured, and with it the false prophet who had performed the signs on its behalf. With these signs he had deluded those who had received the mark of the beast and worshiped its image. The two of them were thrown alive into the fiery lake of burning sulfur. The rest were killed with the sword coming

out of the mouth of the rider on the horse, and all the birds gorged themselves on their flesh. (Revelation 19:19–21)

Though the Antichrist and the False Prophet have been consigned to the lake of fire, Satan still awaits the Final Judgment. We will discuss his fate in the next chapter. For now, it's enough to know that the Lord Jesus and the army of believers will be victorious, and the forces of the unholy trinity will be destroyed. And I cannot wait for that day!

I once read a story about an elderly man, a man of simple faith, who was reading the book of Revelation. A skeptic saw what the old man was reading and decided to make fun of him. "Hey, old-timer," the skeptic said, "that's a strange book you're reading. Are you sure you understand what it means?"

The old man replied, "It means God wins."

That's all we need to know: God wins.

In Revelation 16:17, immediately after the final battle, the seventh angel pours out his bowl of God's wrath upon the air. Out of the temple of heaven comes a voice from the throne, saying, "It is done!" But those words do not mean that the judgment of God has ended. Instead, we now see the final phase of God's judgment against wickedness upon the earth.

Immediately, waves of destruction rain down upon the planet. Lightning flashes from horizon to horizon. Thunder deafens the human race. The ground shakes like no other earthquake in human history. The Richter scale can't measure it—the power of this quake is off the charts. Jerusalem splits into three parts, and the cities of the world collapse into rubble. Mountains implode; islands sink beneath the sea. Massive chunks of hail blast the earth, killing countless human beings.

It is spiritually and emotionally painful to describe this time of judgment. I think of my friends, family members, neighbors, people I've talked to around the world, and I wonder—what if they are left on this earth to go through the horrors of that day?

The people who suffer the awful judgment of God's wrath are no different from you and me—except in one regard: we accepted the Lord's grace; they rejected His grace. It is only by the forgiving grace of God that we have escaped the judgment they will suffer. You and I are saved by the mercy of God alone. None of our good works could ever withstand the justice of a holy God.

Though I am grateful to be eternally secure in God's hands, I grieve for all those who will be alive in those days when God's wrath is poured out upon the earth. I grieve for all those who will go into eternity without Christ. To me, Revelation 16 is the most tragic chapter in the Bible. Here we see the ultimate collision between God's justice and man's disobedience.

I don't gloat over the judgment of God. No one could take pleasure in these scenes of destruction. God Himself does not gloat over the fate of the wicked (Ezekiel 33:11). He is not willing that any should perish, but that all should come to repentance (2 Peter 3:9). Yet He will not overrule our free will. If we choose judgment, then judgment it shall be.

No one has to suffer eternal separation from God. The victory over sin and death has already been won. Jesus has paid the price of our redemption—and He will triumph over Satan.

Sometimes it appears that evil is winning, but we don't walk by sight. We see with eyes of faith. As you watch the news from the Middle East, as you hear of wars and rumors of wars, as you see an increase in beheadings and other horrors, don't doubt the Lord's promise. Our victory is assured. We have God's Word on it.

In the early 1800s, before the invention of the telegraph, England had a communication system called the semaphore line. Using a system of flags and telescopes, messages could be relayed from tower to tower across the length and breadth of England.

In July 1812, the Duke of Wellington led his forces into battle against the French in Salamanca, Spain. News of the battle was delivered to the naval port in Plymouth, England. The commander of the port, Captain Robert Calder, took the message from the courier and climbed the semaphore tower. Using signal flags, he would send the message to the next tower in line, and the message would be relayed to London, two hundred miles away.

Captain Calder began transmitting: "Wellington defeated—"

Just then, the fog rolled in, interrupting the message. The bank of fog continued to shroud the port for most of the day. Meanwhile, those two words, "Wellington defeated," were relayed from tower to tower all the way to London.

When the people of London heard of the Duke of Wellington's defeat, they panicked. Businessmen sold their government bonds. Fortunes were lost.

Back in Plymouth, the fog lifted. Captain Calder transmitted the complete message: "Wellington defeated the French at Salamanca." Despair turned to celebration![4]

So it is with you and me. Jesus has won the victory. Satan is a defeated foe. The Battle of Armageddon has not yet been fought—yet the Lord has declared, "It is done!"

Never surrender to panic or despair. Our Lord will return like a thief, when we least expect Him. Be vigilant. Be prepared. Be faithful.

When He returns, will you be ready?

SIX

COMING SOON

LET'S BEGIN this chapter with a quiz.

Question: What are the four chapters in the Bible in which Satan and his work are completely absent?

Give up?

Answer: The first two and the last two—Genesis 1 and 2, and Revelation 21 and 22.

Satan raises his ugly serpent's head in Genesis 3, and he battles God and bedevils the human race throughout the Bible. Finally in Revelation 20, God consigns Satan to the lake of fire.

Satan hates the Bible—and there are no two books of the Bible he hates more than Genesis and Revelation. Why? Because in Genesis, God pronounces Satan's death sentence. And in Revelation, the sentence is carried out.

Why do increasing numbers of false teachers tell us that Genesis is a myth and Revelation is a mystery? I'm convinced that Satan himself is behind this false teaching. Satan wants to keep us away from Genesis and Revelation, because he wants to hide the truth from us—the truth that he is already a condemned spirit.

This Battle of Armageddon and the defeat of Satan are precipitated by one all-important prophetic event: the Second Coming of Christ.

The promise of the Lord's Second Coming is repeated several times: "I am coming soon. Hold on to what you have, so that no one will take your crown" (Revelation 3:11). "Look, I am coming soon! Blessed is the one who keeps the words of the prophecy written in this scroll" (Revelation 22:7). "Look, I am coming soon! My reward is with me, and I will give to each person according to what they have done" (Revelation 22:12). "He who testifies to these things says, 'Yes, I am coming soon.' Amen. Come, Lord Jesus" (Revelation 22:20).

When that promise is fulfilled, and the Lord returns, it will be the greatest day in history. On that day, the oppressive rule of Satan ends and the glorious reign of Jesus begins. That moment is described in Revelation 11, when the seventh trumpet sounds, and the voices from heaven—the voices of the angels, the elders, and all who have been redeemed—shout:

> The kingdom of the world has become
>> the kingdom of our Lord and of his Messiah,
>> and he will reign for ever and ever. . . .

> We give thanks to you, Lord God Almighty,
>> the One who is and who was,
> because you have taken your great power
>> and have begun to reign.

The nations were angry,
    and your wrath has come.
The time has come for judging the dead,
    and for rewarding your servants the prophets
and your people who revere your name,
    both great and small—
and for destroying those who destroy the earth.
(Revelation 11:15, 17–18)

On that day, the prophecy of Isaiah will at last be fulfilled, as Jesus establishes His government over the entire world:

For to us a child is born,
    to us a son is given,
    and the government will be on his shoulders.
And he will be called
    Wonderful Counselor, Mighty God,
    Everlasting Father, Prince of Peace.
Of the greatness of his government and peace
    there will be no end.
He will reign on David's throne
    and over his kingdom,
establishing and upholding it
    with justice and righteousness
    from that time on and forever. (Isaiah 9:6–7)

Isaiah wrote those words seven hundred years before Jesus was born. More than two thousand years after Jesus was born, we still await the fulfillment of that prophecy. But here in the book of Revelation, we see how that prophecy will be fulfilled. We see that Messiah will reign, and the government will be on His shoulders forever and ever.

We also see the reign of Jesus, the everlasting King, in the shout of the heavenly multitude in Revelation 19:

> Hallelujah!
> For our Lord God Almighty reigns.
> Let us rejoice and be glad
> and give him glory!
> For the wedding of the Lamb has come,
> and his bride has made herself ready. (vv. 6–7)

The eternal reign of Jesus the Messiah will begin with an event that is described in Revelation 19. This event is called the Marriage Supper of the Lamb.

THE MARRIAGE SUPPER OF THE LAMB

The Marriage Supper of the Lamb is like no wedding feast you have ever attended. In our weddings today, the bride is the focus of attention—and rightly so. When I perform weddings, I say to the bride, "Honey, this is your day. I will do whatever you ask me, within reason. It's your day, and I want everything to be perfect for you."

But at the Marriage Supper of the Lamb, it will be the Groom's coronation day—the day He is enthroned as King of kings and Lord of lords.

In the first century, when John wrote Revelation, most Jewish weddings had three stages. In the first stage, the father of the bride and the father of the groom would write a binding agreement called a *ketubah*. For example, when Mary and Joseph were betrothed to each other, they were man and wife in every sense except living together and consummating the marriage. Their marriage contract was so binding that it would take a legal divorce to break their betrothal.

In the second stage, the father of the groom returns home and he and his son, the groom, prepare a room in the home where the bride will live after they are married. After the extra room in the parents' house is ready, the groom's father goes to the house of the bride's father, and he brings the bride and presents her to his son. This stage is called the *chuppah*.

In the third stage, the groom's father hosts the wedding feast—a time of celebration, music, dancing, and joy.

In a similar way, the church is "married" to the Bridegroom, Jesus Christ. This marriage is an *arranged* marriage, just as ancient Jewish marriages were arranged. When did the Father arrange the marriage between His Son and the bride? Before the foundation of the earth. You were spoken for long before you existed. The Lord chose you—you did not choose Him. He called you and predestined you, and He brought you to Himself to be His bride. There is a three-stage process whereby our marriage to the Bridegroom takes place:

In the first stage, the Holy Spirit comes to us and opens our spiritual eyes, removing our blindness. And make no mistake—every one of us is born spiritually blind. We don't see our need of salvation and forgiveness. But when the Holy Spirit opens our eyes, He convicts us of sin. Once we realize we need a Savior, we repent and invite Him to take control of our lives. At that moment, the Lord adopts us into His family and writes our names in the book of life.

I once spoke at a funeral service for a young woman in our church. The fact that she passed away so young made the loss all the more painful for her grieving loved ones. I had prepared a message of hope—but as I got up to speak, I felt the Lord urging me to say something I hadn't planned to say.

"Many Christians struggle with a lack of assurance," I said. "They can point to the moment they received Jesus as their Lord and Savior, but now they wonder if they are still saved. They wonder if there's some unconfessed sin in their lives that has canceled out their salvation. Maybe God has reopened the book of life and erased their name.

"If that is your struggle today, I want you to know that God does not write our name in the book of life in pencil. He does not erase our name every time we sin, then write it back in when we repent. That is not what the Bible teaches. When God writes our name in the book of life, He writes it in the precious blood of Jesus. There is no ink that is more permanent and indelible than the blood of our Savior." That's the first stage: He writes our names in the book of life.

The second stage: the Lord comes for the bride, the body of genuine believers. This is the event we called the Rapture. Notice how this stage differs from the second stage of a Jewish wedding. In a Jewish wedding, the father of the groom goes to fetch the bride and bring her back to his son. But in our case, the Groom—the Lord Jesus—comes to fetch His church and take her to His Father's house. There, He presents His bride to God the Father.

Isn't that a wonderful thought? Jesus comes back to earth at the Rapture and calls the church to meet Him in the air. Then He takes us home to meet the Father face-to-face. The very thought of that day should fill us to overflowing with joy. I can't wait for that day!

The third stage: we celebrate the Marriage Supper of the Lamb. That will be the greatest celebration the universe has ever known. Imagine the guest list: Abraham and Sarah. Moses. Joshua. King David. Elijah, Elisha, Isaiah, and Jeremiah. All the apostles, including dear old Paul—and John the Evangelist, the author of Revelation.

The Marriage Supper will not be like the dinner parties we're all familiar with, where you get dressed up, eat a sumptuous dinner, mingle and chat for a few hours, then everybody goes home. You'll never have to leave the Marriage Supper of the Lamb, because you will *be* home.

In Bible times, Middle Eastern wedding feasts lasted for as long as the father of the groom could afford. When he ran out of food and wine, the feast was over. In those days, it was not the father of the bride who wept but the father of the groom—because he got stuck with the bill. A father of modest means might afford a one-day feast; a prosperous father might afford a three-day celebration; a truly wealthy father might throw a party lasting a week or two. A king might celebrate the wedding of the prince for a month or more.

What sort of wedding feast can our God afford? At what point will His hospitality run dry? When will His stockroom and wine cellar be exhausted?

I believe the Marriage Supper of the Lamb will go on and on throughout eternity. The celebration will never end. A million years from now, the party will still be new and fresh and exciting, and the joy will be never-ending. When I think of the Marriage Supper of the Lamb, I get so excited, I have to praise God! I have to shout to Him, raise my hands to Him, clap for Him, and weep tears of joy. If your spirits are low and your faith is dragging, take heart! Be encouraged—because you have an engraved invitation to the Marriage Supper of the Lamb.

The next words John heard were those of an angel, saying, "Write this: Blessed are those who are invited to the wedding supper of the Lamb! . . . These are the true words of God" (Revelation 19:9). Upon hearing those words, John became so emotionally overwrought that he fell to his knees and began to worship the angel. But the angel said, "Don't do that! I am a fellow servant with you and with your brothers and sisters who hold to the testimony of Jesus. Worship God! For it is the Spirit of prophecy who bears testimony to Jesus" (v. 10).

Some Bible commentators are tough on John for taking leave of his senses and worshipping the angel, but I can hardly blame him. I guarantee, when I see Jesus face-to-face, I am absolutely going to lose it. I'll be an emotional basket case! I'll be weeping and laughing, so giddy with joy I won't know what I'm doing. I imagine that was what John felt.

THE LAMB BECOMES THE SHEPHERD

At the end of Revelation 19, we come to another place where the symbolic images are out of chronological order. In verses 11 through 21, John describes a heavenly Warrior on a white horse, and the rider is called Faithful and True. The Warrior goes to battle against the Antichrist and the kings of the earth—and He is victorious.

Since we have already dealt with the Battle of Armageddon, I want to pause and take a closer look at Jesus, the Rider on the white horse. John describes this heavenly Warrior with imagery similar to his description of Jesus in Revelation 1:12–16. In both descriptions, the eyes of Jesus blaze with fire. He sees everything, from our darkest secrets to our hidden motives. In both descriptions, a sharp sword proceeds from His mouth—a double-edged sword of truth to demolish lies. John tells us the heavenly Warrior wears a robe dipped in blood, and His name is the Word of God. As John wrote in the opening lines of his Gospel, "In the beginning was the Word, and the Word was with God, and the Word was God" (John 1:1).

The Lord's robe is dipped in His own blood. We are reminded of Revelation 7:14, where John sees a throng of people wearing white robes. They are the believers "who have come out of the great tribulation; they have washed their robes and made them white in the blood of the Lamb." One day, we will have robes dipped in the blood of the Lamb, symbolizing the righteousness of our Savior. Our own righteousness won't get us to the back door of heaven, much less earn us a seat at the Marriage Supper of the Lamb. Only the righteousness of Jesus can save us. That's why our robes must be dipped in His blood.

John goes on to describe the redeemed martyrs, quoting the words of the prophet Isaiah. These believers, John writes,

> are before the throne of God
>> and serve him day and night in his temple;
> and he who sits on the throne
>> will shelter them with his presence.
> "Never again will they hunger;
>> never again will they thirst.
> The sun will not beat down on them,"
>> nor any scorching heat.
> For the Lamb at the center of the throne
>> will be their shepherd;
> "he will lead them to springs of living water."
>> "And God will wipe away every tear from their eyes."
>>>>> (Revelation 7:15–17)

This is a beautiful message of hope for all believers. The day will come when our trials will be over, and we will have rest. We will wear white robes of victory, purity, and righteousness, because our robes will be washed in the blood of the Lamb. We will serve God in His temple, and He will shelter us with His presence. Never again will we hunger or thirst or feel the scorching heat of the sun, because the Lamb of God will be our Shepherd. What a privilege it will be when He wipes our tears with His nail-scarred hand.

And notice this beautiful paradox: the Lamb of God will become the Shepherd. The Scriptures are filled with such paradoxes: God became a man. The Lord became a slave. The King became a servant. And the Lamb will be our Shepherd. He will fulfill every line of the Twenty-Third Psalm. Our Shepherd will lead us beside the still waters, restore our souls, and lead us in paths of righteousness. And we will dwell in the house of the Lord forever.

The blood of Christ is the only solution to sin and guilt. Not our performance. Not our rituals. Not our good works. Not the money we give. Only the blood of the Lamb can make us clean. Hebrews 9:22 tells us, "without the shedding of blood there is no forgiveness." Why, then, do we talk so little about the blood of Jesus?

A preacher once told me, "I don't talk about the blood very much. I find that talking about blood offends some people." My friend, if the blood of Jesus offends you, then you need to be offended more often. How can any follower of Christ be offended by the precious blood of Jesus? It is the power to save us, the fountain that cleanses us, and the proof of God's love for us. You cannot be saved by the blood of Christ if you are offended by the blood of Christ.

I recently heard the story of a missionary couple, George and Vera Bajenksi, who worked in Ontario province in Canada. On the morning of February 16, 1989, their phone rang. It was bad news: their son, Ben, had been in an accident near the high school where he was a student.

They drove to the intersection and saw the police cars and an ambulance. A newspaper photographer was taking pictures of a young man lying on the pavement, unmoving. He was surrounded by the largest pool of blood they had ever seen.

Vera Bajenksi clutched her husband's arm and said, "George, Ben went home—home to be with Jesus."

She later recalled wanting to collect all the blood—if there was only some way to put that blood back into her son's body. "That blood," she said, "became the most precious thing in the world because it was life. It belonged in my son, my only son, the one I loved so much."

George Bajenksi was heartbroken to see cars driving through the blood of his son. He wanted to throw his coat over the blood and shout, "You will not drive over the blood of my son!"

But out of their sorrow, George and Vera Bajenksi experienced an amazing insight, which they have shared when talking about the blood of Jesus Christ. They realized that they had caught a glimpse of how God the Father must have felt as His only Son bled and died on the cross of Calvary.[1] By shedding the blood of Jesus on the cross, God spoke to the human race in the strongest language He could find. He paid the highest price He could pay. He appealed to the human race through the language of blood—the precious blood of His only Son. Only by redeeming us with the blood of Jesus could He express how much He loves us.

Give thanks for the blood of the Lamb. Tell everyone you know that His blood has saved you. Never be ashamed of the precious, life-giving blood of Jesus.

THE THOUSAND-YEAR REIGN OF CHRIST

Revelation 20 is one of the most triumphant chapters in the entire Bible. Here we see with our own eyes the fulfillment of the plea in the Lord's Prayer: "Your kingdom come, / your will be done, / on earth as it is in heaven" (Matthew 6:10). In Revelation 20, God's kingdom on earth is finally realized, and for the first time since the Fall, God's will is carried out planet-wide.

Now begins the thousand-year reign of Christ, the Millennium. There are many conflicting views among Bible-believing theologians as to how to interpret the Millennium. As long as the body of Christ does not fight over this issue, it really makes little difference which view of the Millennium you choose.

Over the years there have been three primary interpretations of what the thousand-year reign of Christ will mean. Those three theories are called postmillennialism, amillennialism, and premillennialism.

First, postmillennialism: This view is almost nonexistent today, but it was very popular in the late 1800s and early 1900s—the so-called Progressive Era, a time of rapid social change and social reform. Postmillennialists believed that the Millennium had already begun, that the world was getting better and better, and that it would continue progressing toward a paradise on earth. After two world wars, the atomic bomb, and the rise of global terrorism, it has become increasingly difficult to believe we are currently living under the thousand-year reign of Christ.

Second, amillennialism: This view means there is no literal millennium. When you see the Greek prefix *a-* in front of a word, it means "no." Amillennialists believe the thousand-year period that John writes of in Revelation 20 is a metaphor, not a literal thousand-year span of time. Amillennialists believe that Satan is already bound, locked up in the Abyss, so Satan cannot harm the believer. They believe the thousand-year period in Revelation 20 corresponds to the current "church age." They teach that Christ will return at the end of the church age, administer the Final Judgment, then establish a permanent reign over the new heaven and new earth.

Third, premillennialism: This view says that the Millennium will occur exactly as it is described in Revelation 20. Jesus will come and rule the entire earth from Jerusalem, establishing a thousand-year reign of peace. This is the most common view among evangelical Christians.

Now, I confess that I don't hold any of these three views. I have my own interpretation. I call it "panmillennialism." I define *panmillennialism* this way: I'm just going to wait and see how it pans out. At some point in history, all the events in Revelation 20 will be fulfilled, and we will know exactly which view is correct.

In our previous chapter, we saw the defeat of Satan's schemes at the Battle of Armageddon. The Antichrist and the False Prophet are thrown into the lake of fire—but Satan still awaits his ultimate doom. Here, John writes:

And I saw an angel coming down out of heaven, having the key to the Abyss and holding in his hand a great chain. He seized the dragon, that ancient serpent, who is the devil, or Satan, and bound him for a thousand years. He threw him into the Abyss, and locked and sealed it over him, to keep him from deceiving the nations anymore until the thousand years were ended. After that, he must be set free for a short time. (Revelation 20:1–3)

John describes Satan in vivid terms—the Dragon, the ancient serpent (a reference to the tempter in the Garden of Eden), the devil, and Satan. The name *Satan* is a Hebrew word meaning "an adversary."[2] This fallen angel is the enemy of our souls. As Peter said, "Be alert and of sober mind. Your enemy the devil prowls around like a roaring lion looking for someone to devour" (1 Peter 5:8).

One of the ways our adversary tries to hinder our effectiveness for the Lord is by tempting us to compromise. Sometimes the voice of temptation comes in the form of a whisper in our thoughts. At other times, the temptation to compromise may come from other people: "Don't be so dogmatic. Don't say that Jesus is the only way to God—that kind of talk makes you sound intolerant. Don't talk about the blood of Jesus—you'll only offend people. Don't talk about sin—it makes you sound judgmental." Whether the voice comes from within or without, the temptation to compromise God's Word comes not from God but from Satan. Don't listen to it.

John says that he sees the believers whom God has appointed as judges. He sees the souls of martyrs who were beheaded because of their testimony for Jesus and the gospel. They refused to worship the Antichrist or receive the mark of the beast. They were resurrected to reign with Christ for a thousand years.

Next, we come to the best part of Revelation 20—the final destruction of Satan, at the end of the thousand-year period:

> When the thousand years are over, Satan will be released from his prison and will go out to deceive the nations in the four corners of the earth—Gog and Magog—and to gather them for battle. In number they are like the sand on the seashore. They marched across the breadth of the earth and surrounded the camp of God's people, the city he loves. But fire came down from heaven and devoured them. And the devil, who deceived them, was thrown into the lake of burning sulfur, where the beast and the false prophet had been thrown. They will be tormented day and night for ever and ever. (vv. 7–10)

John speaks of Gog and Magog, a term from Ezekiel 38, a prophecy of the Lord's victory over the hostile nations of the world. At the end of the Millennium, Satan will be released from the Abyss, and he will go out among the nations to incite them to battle. All these nations have been at peace for a thousand years, but Satan will gather them together—and John says their numbers will be so great, they will be like sands on the seashore, surrounding Jerusalem, the city God loves. And God will rain down fire from heaven to engulf Israel's enemies.

Then Satan the deceiver will meet the fate that was prophesied for him in Genesis 3:15. Jesus, the descendant of Eve, will crush the head of the serpent, who is Satan. Our adversary will be thrown into the lake of fire, where the Antichrist and the False Prophet have already been imprisoned for a thousand years.

Next, John describes how God is going to judge the world:

> Then I saw a great white throne and him who was seated on it. The earth and the heavens fled from his presence, and there was no place for them. And I saw the dead, great and small, standing before the throne, and books were opened. Another book was opened, which is the book of life. The dead were judged according to what they had done as recorded in the books. The sea gave up the dead that were in it, and death and Hades gave up the dead that were in them, and each person was judged according to what they had done. Then death and Hades were thrown into the lake of fire. The lake of fire is the second death. Anyone whose name was not found written in the book of life was thrown into the lake of fire. (Revelation 20:11–15)

We will all face that day, and each of us will fall into one group or the other. Who are the two groups that will be judged on that day? Will it be the nice people and the mean people? The good people and the bad people? The people with good doctrine and the people with bad doctrine? No. None of these differences will matter in the Final Judgment. There will only be one factor that divides these two groups: those whose names are written in the book of life—and those whose names are *not* written in the book of life.

God's judgment is neither arbitrary nor unfair. He will judge based on evidence that is recorded in the books. Remember, John said he saw that the books were opened, and the dead were judged according to what they had done, as recorded in the books. Everything we do and say is in those books. That's why Jesus tells us, "Everyone will have to give account on the day of judgment for every empty word they have spoken" (Matthew 12:36).

Now, I don't know if God has literal books in heaven in which our deeds are being recorded moment by moment. These books may be a metaphor to describe some unknown mechanism God has for recording our words and actions. Albert Einstein described time as a fourth dimension in which the past, present, and future are all equally real. In a sympathy letter to the widow of a recently departed friend, Einstein wrote, "Now he has departed from this strange world a little ahead of me. That means nothing. People like us, who believe in physics, know that the distinction between past, present, and future is only a stubbornly persistent illusion."[3] So it may be that the recording of our words and deeds is imprinted on the fabric of the universe, and God can simply show us the complete timeline of our existence, from birth to death.

How would you feel if you discovered that God could play back your entire life—every sinful act, every careless word, everything you ever did that you thought was secret and hidden? What if it was all used against you on the Day of Judgment? Isn't that a chilling thought?

But there's another book—the book of life. If your name is

written in the book of life, then nothing that is contained in those other books can be used against you. If your name is written in the book of life, then you have nothing to fear.

But if your name is not written in that book, you have nothing to hope for.

Jesus said that on the Day of Judgment, many stand before Him, pleading, "Lord, Lord"—yet they are *false* disciples. Jesus said:

> Not everyone who says to me, "Lord, Lord," will enter the kingdom of heaven, but only the one who does the will of my Father who is in heaven. Many will say to me on that day, "Lord, Lord, did we not prophesy in your name and in your name drive out demons and in your name perform many miracles?" Then I will tell them plainly, "I never knew you. Away from me, you evildoers!" (Matthew 7:21–23)

People will stand before Jesus, saying, "Lord, Lord, did I not attend church?" And Jesus will answer, *Your name is not written in the book of life.*

People will say, "Lord, Lord, did I not do charity work?" *Your name is not written in the book of life.*

People will say, "Lord, Lord, wasn't I kind to others?" *Your name is not written in the book of life.*

People will say, "Lord, Lord, didn't I give money to the church?" *Your name is not written in the book of life.*

People will say, "Lord, Lord, didn't I have the right doctrine?" *Your name is not written in the book of life.*

You may ask, "How can I be sure that my name is written in the book of life?" Jesus said, "Only the one who does the will of my Father who is in heaven." Is Jesus saying we must live a sinless life in order to be saved? Of course not. Our righteousness cannot save us. Only the righteousness of Jesus can save. The will of the Father is that we commit our lives to the Lord Jesus Christ. Then, whenever we sin, we confess our sin and repent, and He restores us to a full relationship with Him.

You can know with assurance that your name is written in the book of life. I know that my name is written there because I came to Jesus as a sinner, repented of my sins, and received Him as my Lord and Savior. Jesus said that when you do that, your name is written in the book of life. No one can erase it.

Whenever someone comes to me and says, "I *hope* my name is written in the book of life, but I'm not really sure"—I say, "Well, let's make sure right now, once and for all, so you'll never have to wonder again." I want you to be absolutely confident that the instant after you close your eyes in death, you will see Jesus face-to-face. I want you to know that your name is inscribed in that book in the indelible lettering of the Lord's own blood.

Confess to Him that you are a sinner, repent of your sins, and receive Jesus, once and for all, as your Lord and your Savior. Ask Him to write your name in His book in His own precious blood. Then live every day for Him. When the Day of Judgment comes, you'll have no reason to be ashamed. Your name is in the book.

WE WILL SEE HIM FACE-TO-FACE

One of the great blessings and benefits of studying the book of Revelation is that it alters the way we look at our lives and live our lives in the here and now. Revelation fills us with a sense of expectation and hope—and our hope for the future impacts the daily decisions we make in the present. The Christian who believes in the reality of heaven lives differently from the worldly person who believes only in this earthly existence.

There's an acronym for the worldly view of life: YOLO—You Only Live Once. For the believer, that's simply not true. You live once, you die—and then there's the resurrection! If you know the Lord, you will live forever with Him. This present life is nothing but a dress rehearsal for the life to come. You look forward with eagerness and joy to the new heaven and the new earth that are yet to come. And the best part of heaven is Jesus Himself.

In the last chapter of Revelation, Jesus says three times, "I am coming soon" (Revelation 22:7, 12, 20). Clearly, the Lord wants us to expect His return. He wants us to look forward to that day when we finally see Him face-to-face. As the apostle Paul said, "For now we see only a reflection as in a mirror; then we shall see face to face. Now I know in part; then I shall know fully, even as I am fully known" (1 Corinthians 13:12).

Have you ever considered what it will be like to see Jesus face-to-face? Nobody has ever seen the face of God. Even Moses, who went up on the mountain and received the Law directly from God Himself, has never seen God's face. In Exodus 33, Moses pleads with God, "Now show me your glory." God replies, "You cannot see my face, for no one may see me and live" (vv. 18, 20).

But then the Lord tells Moses, "There is a place near me where you may stand on a rock. When my glory passes by, I will put you in a cleft in the rock and cover you with my hand until I have passed by. Then I will remove my hand and you will see my back; but my face must not be seen" (vv. 21–23). So Moses glimpsed the glory of God, but he never saw God's face.

When we are united with the Lord in heaven, we will see Him face-to-face. Can you imagine the emotions of that moment? Can you imagine what it will feel like to see your beloved Lord for the first time?

Years ago, I heard the story of William Montague Dyke, the son of a prominent member of the British Parliament. He was engaged to a beautiful young lady, the daughter of a renowned British admiral. They were to be married on October 12, 1900.

But young William had never seen the face of his bride. Though he was deeply in love with her, he had no idea what she looked like. Why? Because at the age of ten, William had been injured in an accident that caused him to be blind. Despite his handicap, he had studied at Cambridge and had graduated with honors. He fell in love with his beloved bride-to-be because of her voice, her touch, and the kindness of her heart.

After they announced their engagement, one of England's most prominent eye surgeons approached William and said, "There's an experimental procedure I have performed a number of times with some success. William, I believe I can help you see again."

William agreed to undergo the surgery, and he asked the doctor to attend the wedding and remove the bandages at the altar.

William explained, "I want the first sight I see to be the vision of my beloved, coming down the aisle to be my wife."

On the appointed day, William stood at the altar, waiting for his bride. Next to him was the surgeon. As the organist played the wedding march, the surgeon cut the bandages from William's eyes.

William looked—and he *saw*.

"At last," he said as he gazed upon the beautiful, shining face of his beloved for the very first time. "At last!"[4]

When we get to heaven, it will not be the bride but the Bridegroom we will see for the very first time. We have been blind all our lives, seeing through a glass darkly, unable to see the face of our Lord and Savior—but on that day, we will see Him face-to-face. And John tells us that "we shall be like him, for we shall see him as he is" (1 John 3:2).

Our own faces will shine with joy as we say, "At last, at last!"

Are you ready for that day?

Jesus said, "Yes, I am coming soon!" For those who love Him, who eagerly look forward to His appearing, those words are a blessed promise. For those who have not received Him, those words are a warning—and an invitation.

Don't wait. Don't put it off. Receive Him into your life—and He will receive you into heaven. There is no time to lose.

He is coming soon.

PART 4

THE NEW HEAVEN AND THE NEW EARTH

Setting Our Minds on Things Above

SEVEN

A VISION OF HEAVEN

IN FEBRUARY 2015, the Internet news site Salon posted an article called "Ten Reasons the Christian Heaven Would Actually Be Hell." Isn't that amazing? There's so much hate on the Internet that even heaven gets a bad review!

"The closer you look," said the author, "the more the Bible's version of paradise seems like another version of eternal torture." Here are some of the reasons this writer gives for saying that heaven would be hell:

First, everyone in heaven would be perfect, so we would all be the same. "Perfect means finished and complete," the writer explained. "It means there's no room for improvement—for change and growth. Perfection is sterile, in every sense of the word." Who wants to live forever with a bunch of perfect people? Who wants to live in a world where no one would ever lie to you, steal from you, or murder you?

But where does this writer get the idea that perfection means sameness? God made each of us as unique human beings, with a unique set of personality traits. The fact that we will be morally and spiritually perfect in heaven doesn't mean that we will all be cookie-cutter creations. We will still be the unique, one-of-a-kind individuals God created us to be, yet gloriously and wonderfully perfected.

Second, this writer says that heaven will be boring because "most exhilarating experiences require risk: flying down a ski slope almost out of control, jumping out of airplanes, racing cars, surfing, performing." If it's excitement you want, I truly believe that heaven will be a place of unimaginable exhilaration, where we will be able to visit the far reaches of our vast universe, experience emotions we can't even imagine right now, and engage our resurrection minds and resurrection bodies in adventures that are infinitely beyond anything we have ever known in this life.

Third, this writer claims that "free will ceases to exist" in heaven. The writer explains, "In heaven there is no sin, no option to sin, and so, by Christianity's own definition, no free will."[1] No free will in heaven? I've never seen that verse in the Bible. Where do the Scriptures tell us that God takes away our free will once we get to heaven?

We will be free in heaven—more free than we have ever been during our earthly lives. But in heaven we will have our resurrection minds and resurrection bodies, and we will understand all things so clearly and completely that it would make no rational sense to choose sin instead of choosing God.

Toddlers, who have limited knowledge and limited understanding, will drink poison and play in the street simply because they don't know any better. If you take away their poison and yank them out of the street, they think you're being mean for taking away their free will. But when that child becomes an adult, he no longer wants to drink poison or play in the street, because his knowledge is more complete. In the same way, we will have free will in heaven, but we will no longer want to do the sinful, foolish, self-destructive things that once seemed so appealing to us.

The writer goes on—offering reason after reason that no person in his or her right mind should ever want to go to heaven. And the rest of those reasons are just as specious as the ones I discussed here.

Now consider this: Doesn't this sound like exactly the kind of propaganda you would expect from Satan? Doesn't this sound just like our adversary's voice: "Why would anybody want to go to a miserable place like heaven? All the really cool people are going to hell. Heaven is for losers and squares. Take it from me—hell is the place to be!"

So if you think heaven is going to be a miserable, boring experience—I want you to know that you've been duped. Satan has sold you a bill of goods. It's time you learned what the Bible *really* teaches about heaven.

Randy Alcorn, founder of Eternal Perspective Ministries, recalls a conversation he had with a pastor. This pastor told him, "Whenever I think about heaven, it makes me depressed. I'd rather just cease to exist when I die."

Alcorn was shocked. "Why?"

"I can't stand the thought of that endless tedium," the pastor said. "To float around in the clouds with nothing to do but strum a harp—it's all so terribly boring. Heaven doesn't sound much better than hell. I'd rather be annihilated than spend eternity in a place like that."

Alcorn had to shake his head and wonder, "Where did this Bible-believing, seminary-educated pastor get such a view of heaven? Certainly not from Scripture."[2]

It's shocking how many Bible-believing *Christians* are afraid of the life to come. If you are concerned about being bored in heaven, then I have good news: You are about to discover how exciting and wonderful heaven will be.

IMPACT THE PRESENT—FOCUS ON HEAVEN

In the book of Revelation, the Lord Jesus gives John a vision of heaven. It's a vision of comfort and encouragement for everyone who is burdened by the sufferings of this life. You won't be floating on the clouds, strumming a harp. You won't be a robot. You won't be bored for all eternity. You won't be a disembodied spirit floating around in some strange dimension. Heaven will be filled with all the excitement you could ever want.

Jesus said, "I go to prepare a *place* for you." Not a cloud. Not a dimension. A *place*. Heaven is a *real place*, and we will live there in our glorified resurrection bodies.

The place Jesus is preparing for us is the new heaven and the new earth, the domain of God, the dwelling place of His people. And the capital city of the new heaven is the New Jerusalem. John's vision describes in breathtaking detail the place where we will live forever. The vision of heaven we find in Revelation is designed to fill us with anticipation for the life to come and to comfort us in our trials. The promise of heaven should motivate us to live each day for the Lord. Peter reminds us that we ought to live lives of holiness and godliness because "we are looking forward to a new heaven and a new earth, where righteousness dwells" (2 Peter 3:13).

In *Mere Christianity*, C. S. Lewis explains why the future hope of heaven motivates us to live boldly for Christ in the here and now:

> A continual looking forward to the eternal world is not (as some modern people think) a form of escapism or wishful thinking, but one of the things a Christian is meant to do. It does not mean that we are to leave the present world as it is. If you read history you will find that the Christians who did most for the present world were just those who thought most of the next. The Apostles themselves, who set on foot the conversion of the Roman Empire, the great men who built up the Middle Ages, the English evangelicals who abolished the slave trade, all left their mark on earth, precisely because their minds were occupied with heaven. It is since Christians have largely ceased to think of the other world that they have become so ineffective in this. Aim at heaven and you will get earth "thrown in:" Aim at earth and you will get neither.[3]

One of the great tragedies of the church today is that there is so little preaching on heaven. Most of the preaching we hear in the American church is focused on the problems of *this* life, the blessings of *this* life, on how to get the most out of *this* life. Heaven gets very little mention from our pulpits today.

How different are the priorities of today's churches from the priorities of God's Word. The Bible mentions heaven more than five hundred times. The book of Revelation mentions heaven more than fifty times. Yet many churches these days seem to avoid the subject of heaven almost entirely. They are caught up in society's mad pursuit for instant gratification and narcissistic self-indulgence. Instead of rightly dividing the Word of Truth, all too many churches deliver motivational pep talks. Ministers are becoming audience pleasers instead of God pleasers.

The more we focus our attention on this life, the more meaningless this life becomes. But the more we focus on the wonders of heaven, the more wonderful this life becomes. When I hear someone talking excitedly about heaven, I know that person is truly saved. One of the surest indicators of genuine salvation is a sense of excitement and expectation about heaven. Jesus said, "For where your treasure is, there your heart will be also" (Matthew 6:21). So if your treasure is in heaven, then your heart is in heaven as well.

A focus on heaven produces godly characteristics in our lives right here, right now. A focus on heaven brings us joy and comfort in the midst of trials. A focus on heaven places our earthly pain, suffering, and persecution into an eternal perspective. A focus on heaven helps us to persevere against temptation and sin.

Today, you may be carrying the weight of a Steinway piano on your back. It might be a load of guilt. It might be a load of suffering and pain. It might be a load of worry about the future or heartbreak over a painful loss. Whatever the weight that drags you down today, a vision of heaven will lift your burden.

If you have been avoiding all that the Bible teaches about

heaven, then you have been missing out on one of the great blessings of the Christian faith. The hope of heaven is one of the great expectations of our faith, enabling us to soar above the problems and frustrations of this earthly life.

In Revelation 4, God graciously opens a door into heaven and gives John the extraordinary privilege of seeing what heaven will be like. Why does God give John this vision of heaven? I believe it's so that you and I will lose any fear we might have about the afterlife. God wants us to be filled with joy and excitement about our future home in heaven. John writes:

> After this I looked, and there before me was a door standing open in heaven. And the voice I had first heard speaking to me like a trumpet said, "Come up here, and I will show you what must take place after this." At once I was in the Spirit, and there before me was a throne in heaven with someone sitting on it. (vv. 1–2)

This is John's first impression of heaven. I'm reminded of the story of an elderly couple who died at the same time and entered heaven together. As they were walking around heaven and looking at all the beautiful sights, the husband turned to his wife and said, "Honey, if I had known how beautiful heaven would be, I wouldn't have eaten all that oatmeal you gave me."

And though the story is not true, it makes a valid statement: if we only realized how wonderful heaven will be, we wouldn't cling to our earthly lives so tightly. We might stop eating healthy oatmeal and start eating more artery-clogging bacon and sausage if doing so would get us to heaven any sooner. (But eat your oatmeal anyway.)

John describes his first glimpse of heaven—he sees a throne with Someone seated on it. We should not interpret this image to mean that God is a man sitting on a piece of furniture, like an earthly monarch. The image of the throne is symbolic, not literal. It symbolizes the power and authority of our God. He is the Creator and Ruler of this vast universe of time and space, galaxies and stars, planets and moons, atoms and quarks.

Most important of all, the Lord deserves to be enthroned in our hearts. This image of God on the throne of heaven is good news for you and me. If we will step down from the throne of our hearts and put the Lord Jesus Christ on the throne instead, He will come into our lives with strength and might. He will take over and rule, bringing us power and joy in the midst of our trials.

John's first glimpse of heaven shows us that the throne of God is the fixed center of the universe. It is the immovable point of reference for all of time and space. It is much like the North Star that guides navigators on their ocean voyages. It is the hub around which the entire universe revolves.

We have a tendency to watch the news and think, *Everything is out of control.* But when God looks at the world, He doesn't think, *Oh my, what am I going to do? The world is in such a mess; I'll never be able to fix it!* No, God is patient, God is in control, and God has a plan for the entire universe. Everything—even our sin, even war and terrorism and all the sorrows of this world—are accounted for in His plan. And the book of Revelation shows us that these events are proceeding according to God's timetable.

THE THREE HEAVENS

Most Christians seem to have a hazy notion of heaven as a place up in the sky, "way beyond the blue."[4] But that is not how the Bible describes heaven.

In fact, many Christians are surprised to discover that the Bible actually talks about three different heavens. And they are even more surprised to discover that the first heaven, as described in the Bible, is not the domain of God. The first heaven is where Satan dwells.

Paul talks about the first heaven in Ephesians 6:12: "For our struggle is not against flesh and blood, but against the rulers, against the authorities, against the powers of this dark world and against *the spiritual forces of evil in the heavenly realms.*" Paul also tells us (in Ephesians 3:10) that the church demonstrates God's "manifold wisdom" (that is, His vast and varied wisdom) to "the rulers and authorities in the heavenly realms." In other words, our faithfulness demonstrates to Satan and the other demons of the first heaven that God's judgment against them is righteous, wise, and just.

We usually think of "heavenly" as referring to things that are good, to things that are of God. But the first heavenly realm is really nothing more or less than the spiritual realm, the invisible domain that is all around us, but which we cannot see. It is the realm of angels and demons, the realm of spiritual powers such as the prince of Greece and the prince of Persia that are mentioned in Daniel 9—demonic "kings" who have authority over nations and kingdoms of the earth.

The second heaven is the universe, the celestial heaven. When you look up at the night sky or see photographs of deep space taken by the Hubble Space Telescope, you are looking at the second heaven.

The third heaven is sometimes referred to in Scripture as "paradise." This is the heaven Jesus spoke of when he told the repentant thief on the cross, "Truly I tell you, today you will be with me in paradise" (Luke 23:43). This is the heaven the apostle Paul spoke of when he says he was "caught up to paradise" where he "heard inexpressible things, things that no one is permitted to tell" (2 Corinthians 12:4). It must have been hard for Paul, who was privileged to experience the indescribable wonders of paradise, to be forbidden to tell anyone what he saw.

But this third heaven, the paradise our spirits go to after we die, is not the final and future heaven, the eternal heaven that Jesus promised to prepare for us. When we as believers die, we go to this third heaven where Jesus is now. When the new heaven comes, the old heaven will be swept away. As John writes in Revelation 21:1, "Then I saw 'a new heaven and a new earth,' for the first heaven and the first earth had passed away, and there was no longer any sea."

Every so often, a new book comes out by someone who supposedly died, went to heaven, and came back. Some of these books are written by Christians; some are not. They frequently hit the bestseller list and have become a publishing subgenre known as "heavenly tourism."

One such book was *The Boy Who Came Back from Heaven: A True Story.* Published in 2010, the book sold more than a million copies and was adapted as a TV movie. It tells the story of

Alex Malarkey, who was severely injured in an automobile accident when he was six years old. The boy was in a coma for two months and his injuries left him paralyzed. Emerging from his coma, he told his parents that an angel had taken him through the gates of heaven.

Today, Alex Malarkey is a teenager, and he still struggles with the aftereffects of brain trauma, though an operation made it possible for him to breathe on his own without a ventilator. In a January 2015 open letter, Alex said:

> I did not go to heaven. . . . I said I went to heaven because I thought it would get me attention. When I made the claims that I did, I had never read the Bible. People have profited from lies, and continue to. They should read the Bible, which is enough. The Bible is the only source of truth. Anything written by man cannot be infallible.[5]

The boy's parents are divorced, and Alex's mother, Beth, is his primary caregiver. Yet the contract for the book was with the boy's father—and Alex and his mother receive no money from the book, not even for his medical needs. Alex and his mother have been trying to tell the world that the so-called true story isn't true at all—but for years, nobody would listen. So a six-year-old boy's fib to get attention was blown up into a *New York Times* Best Seller and a TV movie.

Beth Malarkey recalls how Alex repeatedly tried to tell people that the book was full of lies. When the boy told a pastor that the book was deceptive and needed to be pulled from bookstores, the pastor replied that the book was "blessing people." Beth Malarkey responded that saying a deceptive book "blesses" other people is nothing but a way of justifying wrongdoing. In a blog post, she concluded:

> The ones making money from the book are NOT the ones staying up through the night, struggling for their breath, nor were they the ones at six years old, waking up unable to move or breathe. . . . There are many who are scamming and using the Word of God. . . . Alex did not write the book and it is not blessing him.[6]

The next time you are tempted to read one of these "heavenly tourism" books, remember the words of the boy who supposedly came back from heaven—but didn't: "Read the Bible, which is enough. The Bible is the only source of truth."

And consider this: even if this boy had gone into the presence of Jesus, then came back to tell us what he saw—what place would he be describing? We know for a fact that no one has ever died and gone to the eternal heaven that John writes about in the book of Revelation—let alone come back to tell about it. How do we know that? Because the new heaven and the new earth will not exist until the old heaven and the old earth pass away. That's what John tells us in Revelation 21:1.

So if anyone tells you they have died and have seen our eternal home in heaven, don't believe it. We know from Scripture that it can't possibly be true.

SYMBOLS OF CRYSTAL-CLEAR TRUTH

What does John see when he peers through the doorway into heaven? He continues his description of the heavenly throne room:

> And the one who sat there had the appearance of jasper and ruby. A rainbow that shone like an emerald encircled the throne. Surrounding the throne were twenty-four other thrones, and seated on them were twenty-four elders. They were dressed in white and had crowns of gold on their heads. From the throne came flashes of lightning, rumblings and peals of thunder. In front of the throne, seven lamps were blazing. These are the seven spirits of God. Also in front of the throne there was what looked like a sea of glass, clear as crystal. (Revelation 4:3–6)

John sees Jesus, our great High Priest—and he describes Jesus as having the appearance of gemstones: jasper and ruby. These stones should be interpreted symbolically, not literally. Jasper is a diamond-like white stone that symbolizes the glory and purity of Jesus. The ruby is a blood-red stone symbolizing the sacrificial blood of Jesus, which was shed on the cross. These two stones were worn by the high priest of Israel in Old Testament times, and they symbolized the beginning and the end, the first and the last, the alpha and the omega.

Surrounding the throne is a rainbow, which reminds us of God's faithfulness to His promises. In Genesis 9, after God destroyed the world with the Flood and saved Noah and his family in the ark, He promised, "I establish my covenant with you: Never again will all life be destroyed by the waters of a flood; never again will there be a flood to destroy the earth. . . . I have set my rainbow in the clouds, and it will be the sign of the covenant between me and the earth" (Genesis 9:11, 13).

Rainbows are created when sunlight is reflected by millions of raindrops. A beam of white sunlight enters a raindrop, reflects off the back of the raindrop, and bounces back, bending slightly as it passes through the droplet. When white light is bent, it splits into different wavelengths, producing rainbow bands of color: red-orange-yellow-green-blue-indigo-violet. If you fly over a waterfall in an airplane, you can look down and see rainbows in the shape of complete circles. The rainbows we usually see, however, are in the shape of a semicircle. This is because the ground gets in the way of the raindrops and blocks the bottom half of the rainbow.

Here in Revelation 4, the apostle John describes something that he had probably never seen with his earthly eyes—a rainbow in the shape of a full circle. John describes this rainbow as encircling the throne of God and shining brightly like an emerald. The circular shape of the rainbow symbolizes the eternal nature of God, who has no beginning and no end.

When we reach heaven, we will see Jesus, our great High Priest. As our High Priest, Jesus performs two ministries on our behalf. First, He makes sacrifices for us. He made the perfect sacrifice for our sins when He died in our place on the cross.

Second, he intercedes for us. Right now, Jesus is interceding on your behalf before the Father. Were you aware that the Lord Jesus is continually praying for you and advocating for you before the Father?

There are some people who pray to certain saints, such as the Virgin Mary. I have great respect for Mary, the mother of Jesus, because of her faithfulness and obedience when God selected her to give birth to the Messiah. But Mary is not our High Priest. She cannot intercede for us with the Father, and it does no good to ask her to pray for us. Only Jesus can intercede for us before the Father.

The Scriptures make it clear that no one can intercede for us except Jesus: "For there is one God and one mediator between God and mankind, the man Christ Jesus" (1 Timothy 2:5). And, "Therefore he [Jesus] is able to save completely those who come to God through him, because he always lives to intercede for them" (Hebrews 7:25).

In John 17, we find the High Priestly Prayer of Jesus, which He prayed just hours before He was crucified. In that prayer, He prayed not only for His disciples, but for all who would come after them, including you and me: "My prayer is not for them alone. I pray also for those who will believe in me through their message" (John 17:20). Before Jesus gave His life for us, He was interceding for us. And after He ascended to the Father, He continued to intercede for us. He still intercedes for us today.

Next, notice that around the heavenly throne of God's power and authority stand twenty-four elders. The twenty-four elders are symbolic, and in order to understand the symbolism, we need to compare scripture with scripture. The twenty-four elders are a parallel of the twenty-four priests whom King David ordained to serve in the temple (1 Chronicles 24:1–19). Why is the number twenty-four important?

In both 1 Chronicles and the book of Revelation, the number twenty-four symbolizes the twelve tribes of Israel and the twelve disciples of Jesus. This tells us that in heaven, the true church will be made up of saints from the Old and New Testaments. Many Christians mistakenly think that people in Old Testament times were saved by the Law and the animal sacrifices, whereas people in New Testament times are saved by faith. This is not true. Old Testament saints like Abraham looked forward by faith to the coming of Jesus the Messiah; New Testament saints look back in faith to the sacrifice of the Lord Jesus. But all are justified by faith, not by the works of the Law.

In the book of Revelation, God gives us the symbol of the twenty-four elders to show us that heaven will be populated by saints from both the Old and the New Testaments. We will all be one body of believers in heaven, and we will bow in praise and gratitude to the Lord Jesus Christ.

Next, John describes a scene of awesome power, a visible demonstration of God's authority over the elemental forces of the universe. Lightning arcs across the scene, unleashing explosions of thunder.

John tells us that seven lamps blaze in front of the throne, and these, he says, "are the seven spirits of God." In fact, he refers to the seven spirits of God four times: in Revelation 1:4; 3:1; 4:5; and 5:6. What are these seven spirits of God? Has John changed the number of Persons in the Trinity? No, John is using symbolism again.

These seven lamps of fire represent the sevenfold ministry of the Holy Spirit, as found in Isaiah 11:2: the Spirit of the Lord (His comforting presence), the Spirit of wisdom, the Spirit of understanding, the Spirit of counsel, the Spirit of might, the Spirit of knowledge, and the Spirit of the fear of the Lord. When we surrender to the Lord and yield to His Spirit, He will produce these seven qualities in our lives.

Next, John describes a sea of glass, as clear as crystal—a symbol of the pure, clear truth of the Word of God. Satan wants to keep us from reading, studying, memorizing, and obeying the Word of God, because the pure truth of the Word cleanses and sanctifies. Preachers and teachers who substitute motivational pep talks or pop psychology in place of God's Word are robbing people of God's truth.

Satan is a counterfeiter. He doesn't have a creative bone in his body. He never invents anything himself, but he delights in taking God's creations and twisting them for his purposes. Take, for example, institutions of higher learning.

The first universities in the world were founded by cathedrals and taught by religious clerics—Oxford University, founded in 1096; the University of Paris, around 1150; and Cambridge University, around 1209. In America, Harvard University was founded in 1636 by Puritans; it was named for clergyman John Harvard, and its original mission was to educate young men to be pastors. A Harvard alumnus, a Puritan minister named Cotton Mather, went on to found Yale University in 1701.

All of these institutions of higher learning were founded to teach the Christian faith. But Satan, the counterfeiter, wormed his way into these institutions and replaced godly teachers with ungodly propagandists for worldliness. Today, most universities are strongholds of secularism and atheism. Satan could never create a university, but he often takes the great achievements of Christians and subverts them to his own ends.

Satan even twists the crystal-clear truth of heaven into a lie from hell. The book of Revelation speaks symbolically of God's truth like "a sea of glass, clear as crystal" (4:6). Satan has produced his own counterfeit of God's truth, the New Age practices of "crystal energy" and "crystal healing." Satan has convinced gullible people that crystals of quartz, amethyst, or topaz have power to heal, bring love and riches, or ward off evil. So, instead of seeking the crystal-clear truth of God's Word, superstitious people chase after mythical powers that supposedly reside inside dead minerals.

Don't be fooled by Satan's counterfeits. Seek the crystal clarity of God's truth.

SATAN ENVIES US

Next, John gives us a glimpse of worship in heaven—and once again, his description is laden with symbolism. He writes:

> In the center, around the throne, were four living creatures, and they were covered with eyes, in front and in back. The first living creature was like a lion, the second was like an ox, the third had a face like a man, the fourth was like a flying eagle. Each of the four living creatures had six wings and was covered with eyes all around, even under its wings. Day and night they never stop saying:

"'Holy, holy, holy
is the Lord God Almighty,'
who was, and is, and is to come." (Revelation 4:6–8)

The four angelic creatures with many eyes symbolize their involvement with the judgment of God. When Jesus spoke of God's judgment in the Gospels, He often said that God would send His angels to harvest the wheat and separate the chaff. Angels will be involved in the final judgment, and that's why they are depicted as having many eyes. The eyes symbolize the far-seeing wisdom and swift execution of God's judgment.

The angels continually proclaim, "Holy, holy, holy is the Lord God Almighty, who was, and is, and is to come" (Revelation 4:8). Please don't get the idea that, when we get to heaven, we will do nothing but sing a thousand choruses of "How Great Thou Art." One of the great misconceptions about heaven—a misconception Satan planted by twisting the meaning of God's Word—involves the notion that, in heaven, we will do nothing but chant praises to God, hour after hour, millennium after millennium.

No wonder Jesus called Satan a liar and the father of lies. No wonder Satan is our adversary. He is constantly lying about God's greatest gift—eternity with Him in heaven. Why does Satan lie about heaven? Why does he fill believers with a dread of heaven when the expectation of heaven should be our greatest hope?

The answer is obvious: Satan was thrown out of heaven. He will never be allowed to enter the new heaven. He not only hates God, but he hates us. Why? Because we are going to live forever in heaven—and he is going to be tortured forever in the lake of fire. We will inherit everything Satan lost when he rebelled against God and fell from heaven.

Do you understand what that means? *Satan envies you and me.* He hates us and he wants what we have—the hope of heaven. So he will do everything he can to kill that hope within us. He will lie to us. He will fill us with fear and doubt.

Don't let Satan deceive you about heaven. Remember what Paul said:

> However, as it is written:
>   "What no eye has seen,
>   what no ear has heard,
>   and what no human mind has conceived"—
>   the things God has prepared for those who love
>   him." (1 Corinthians 2:9)

So when Satan comes after you, laugh at him, mock him, taunt him: "Get away from me, Satan! I'm going to heaven and you're not!" It's all right to taunt Satan. Rejoice that Satan envies you, because you are covered by the blood of Jesus Christ—and nothing will save Satan from the torments of hell.

When Jesus hung on the cross and His blood became a cleansing flood for you and me, Satan was excluded. All the angels and all the demons were excluded. Jesus did not die for angels. Jesus died for you and me, the sons and daughters of Adam and Eve. It must drive Satan mad with envy to think that God would send His Son to die for these pitiful human creatures. So Satan continually tries to blind us to the hope of heaven.

That's why it's so important to follow Paul's wise counsel: "Set your minds on things above, not on earthly things" (Colossians 3:2). Don't let Satan set your agenda. Don't let Satan control your thinking. Satan wants to keep you focused on earthly things. Don't listen to him. Set your mind on the things of heaven.

If you are afraid that heaven is going to be boring or unpleasant, consider this: heaven comes from the mind of the same Creator who gave us Yosemite National Park, the Grand Canyon, and Niagara Falls. Just think of all the amazing, beautiful, thrilling places God has created around the world for humanity to enjoy. If there is so much beauty and wonder in a world that is fallen and broken by sin, imagine what heaven will be like! Imagine eternity without sin and suffering! The most awe-inspiring waterfall will seem as impressive as a lawn sprinkler next to the wonders God has prepared for us in heaven.

Have you ever wondered why we live in a universe surrounded by billions of galaxies and stars? Have you ever wondered how many planets and moons there must be circling those distant stars? How would you like to explore the whole universe without any physical limitation? Truly, no eye has seen, no ear has heard, no mind has conceived what God has prepared for us.

Will we continually praise God in heaven? Yes, we will. Will we be standing in a big room around a throne, singing endless praise choruses? Hardly. The throne, remember, is symbolic. It speaks of God being the fixed center of the universe. But God does not sit in one chair in one limited locality. God is everywhere. And wherever we go in the universe, whatever we do as we explore the new heaven, we will be able to speak to Him, thank Him, and praise Him. With each new discovery, with each new wonder, our hearts will leap with praise.

Not only do the angels in heaven give God praise, but the twenty-four elders also give praise to God. The elders represent all of God's saints, both the redeemed of Israel in Old Testament times and the redeemed of the church in New Testament times. John writes:

> Whenever the living creatures give glory, honor and thanks to him who sits on the throne and who lives for ever and ever, the twenty-four elders fall down before him who sits on the throne and worship him who lives for ever and ever. They lay their crowns before the throne and say:
>
> "You are worthy, our Lord and God,
>   to receive glory and honor and power,
> for you created all things,
>   and by your will they were created
>   and have their being." (Revelation 4:9–11)

That will be our hymn of praise when we finally see Jesus and hear His voice. We will be reunited with our loved ones. We'll discover the answers to all the questions that troubled us in our earthly lives. We'll explore the gleaming streets and many mansions of the New Jerusalem. We'll thrill to the wonders of the new earth and the new heaven.

And with every new surprise and delight, we will praise Him again and again.

Words are inadequate to describe heaven. The mind is inadequate to imagine eternity with Jesus. If Jesus is your Lord and Savior, all of eternity and infinity will be yours to explore. And the new heaven and the new earth will resound with the praises of His people.

EIGHT

ALL THINGS NEW

I ONCE HEARD A STORY about a real estate developer who wanted to buy a warehouse. The building had been empty and unused for years, and it was in terrible condition. The walls were covered with graffiti. Vandals had broken the doors, smashed the windows, and strewn trash all around.

The buyer met the owner to tour the property. The owner said, "I apologize for the condition of the warehouse. I plan to fix those doors and windows, and I'm going to put a new coat of paint on the place."

"Don't bother," the buyer said. "I'll take it exactly as is. I'm only interested in the land. I'm going to demolish the building."

That's the way God works, whether He is dealing with an entire universe or a single human soul. When the Lord comes into our lives, He doesn't come to fix a broken window and slap on a new coat of paint. As Paul tells us, "Therefore, if anyone is in Christ, the new creation has come: The old has gone, the new is here!" (2 Corinthians 5:17).

And as we look at Revelation 21 and 22, we see that God, the

Cosmic Real Estate Developer, is not going to patch up the old heaven and the old earth with Band-Aids and baling wire. He's going to take a wrecking ball to the universe and start over from scratch. He's going to destroy the old heaven and earth and replace them with a new heaven and a new earth. In Revelation 21:5, the Lord tells John, "I am making everything new!" This will be the fulfillment of the Old Testament prophecy of Isaiah:

"See, I will create
new heavens and a new earth.
The former things will not be remembered,
nor will they come to mind." (Isaiah 65:17)

And it will be the fulfillment of the New Testament prophecies of Jesus and the apostle Peter:

[Jesus said,] "Heaven and earth will pass away, but my words will never pass away." (Matthew 24:35)

By the same word the present heavens and earth are reserved for fire, being kept for the day of judgment and destruction of the ungodly. . . . That day will bring about the destruction of the heavens by fire, and the elements will melt in the heat. But in keeping with his promise we are looking forward to a new heaven and a new earth, where righteousness dwells. (2 Peter 3:7, 12–13)

As the book of Revelation moves toward its conclusion in

Revelation 21 and 22, we see seven new things come into being as the old order passes away. Those seven new things are:

1. A new heaven;
2. A new earth;
3. A new Holy City, the New Jerusalem;
4. New inhabitants of the city—both Old and New Testament believers;
5. A new paradise, a restored Garden of Eden in the midst of the New Jerusalem;
6. A new Light to illuminate the city; and
7. A new temple. (There will be no temple building in the New Jerusalem; it will be replaced by the new "temple" of the New Jerusalem, which is the living and glorious presence of God the Father and God the Son—Revelation 21:22.)

In these chapters, John gives us a richly detailed picture of the place Jesus is preparing for us right now—the new heaven and the new earth. What will the new heaven and new earth be like? What will eternal life be like in the New Jerusalem? As we fix our eyes on our present and future hope of heaven, we will lose our fear of dying—and gain greater courage and enthusiasm for living.

THE NEW HEAVEN, THE NEW EARTH, AND THE NEW JERUSALEM

John's first glimpse into heaven in Revelation 4 gave us a series of images that were largely symbolic, requiring interpretation. As we turn to Revelation 21, where John describes his vision of the new heaven, the new earth, and the New Jerusalem, we need to apply discernment, because some portions of this chapter are intended to be interpreted symbolically while others are meant literally.

John gives us an interesting detail in Revelation 21:1: "Then I saw 'a new heaven and a new earth,' for the first heaven and the first earth had passed away, and there was no longer any sea." We should not move past that verse without giving serious thought to the phrase "there was no longer any sea." I believe this is a literal description of the new earth. The disappearance of the sea will be a radical change in the structure of the earth that will have profound implications for life on earth.

Science-fiction writer Arthur C. Clarke famously observed, "How inappropriate to call this planet 'Earth' when it is quite clearly 'Ocean.'" Three-quarters of the earth is covered by water; only one-quarter is comprised of land. All life on earth depends on water for survival, and Earth is the only planet we know of where there is sufficient water to sustain life.

Whenever scientists send a robot probe to Mars or some other planet, what is the first thing they look for? Water! They want to know if there might be life there. Water makes life possible—at least, life as we know it. Any planet that has never had water has, by definition, never sustained life.

The fact that the new earth will have no sea is significant. Why? Because when we receive our glorified resurrection bodies, when we become like our resurrected Lord, *we won't need water to survive.* The human body is made up of about 60 percent water. The adult human heart and brain are about 73 percent water. Our bodies use water for cell division, digestion, the removal of waste, regulating body temperature, manufacturing hormones and neuro-transmitters, and delivering oxygen throughout the body in the bloodstream.[1]

But our resurrection bodies will be based on a different life principle than the biological principles of this fallen universe. When astronauts walked on the moon, they had to wear their Earth environment around them in the form of the spacesuit—or they would have died. But in our resurrection bodies, we'll be able to visit the airless moon without spacesuits.

Though I believe we should take John literally when he says "there was no longer any sea," there is probably a deep symbolic meaning in those words as well. John was exiled on an island in the Aegean Sea, completely surrounded by water. When he stood on the shore and looked out over the sea, he longed to be with his loved ones in Ephesus—but the waters formed an impassable barrier.

For John, the sea meant separation. You and I have loved ones we were once close to, yet we are separated from them by death. In the new heaven and the new earth, there will be no death, no separation. The sea of death that separates us will be gone. We'll be united with them and with our Lord forever and ever.

Next, the apostle John describes a sight that must have taken his breath away—and once again, I believe John is describing a literal future reality, not a symbol to be interpreted:

I saw the Holy City, the new Jerusalem, coming down out of heaven from God, prepared as a bride beautifully dressed for her husband. And I heard a loud voice from the throne saying, "Look! God's dwelling place is now among the people, and he will dwell with them. They will be his people, and God himself will be with them and be their God. 'He will wipe every tear from their eyes. There will be no more death' or mourning or crying or pain, for the old order of things has passed away." (Revelation 21:2–4)

The Holy City, the New Jerusalem, is the capital city of the new heaven and the new earth. I believe John wants us to understand that the New Jerusalem is meant to be interpreted literally. That's why he later gives us the exact dimensions of this vast city.

John wrote the book of Revelation in about AD 96, about twenty-six years after the Romans under General Titus destroyed the earthly Jerusalem, including the temple. Jesus had told His disciples before the crucifixion that the temple would be destroyed and "not one stone here will be left on another" (Matthew 24:2; Mark 13:2; Luke 21:6). Exactly as Jesus prophesied, the Romans pried apart all the stones of the temple, searching for gold and other loot.

Can you imagine what a shock it was to the Jews to see their Holy City leveled by the Romans? Can you imagine the horror of seeing their magnificent temple burned, dismantled, and removed from the city skyline? Remember the shock America felt after 9/11—then imagine the emotional throes America would have experienced if all of Washington, DC, had been destroyed by a foreign power: the Capitol, the White House, the Washington Monument, the Lincoln Memorial. Such an event would be burned into our national consciousness for decades. That's what the destruction of Jerusalem was like for the Jews.

When John wrote about the New Jerusalem, the old Jerusalem had been gone for more than a quarter century, yet the collective wound was still fresh. John was saying, in effect, "I know that after all these years, you are still in shock over the destruction of Jerusalem and the temple. But don't worry about the earthly Jerusalem. I have seen the *New* Jerusalem—and it is going to be amazing. When you reach the New Jerusalem, you won't believe your eyes."

I love the current city of Jerusalem. I have visited there a number of times. I have friends there, and it is a beautiful city. There's no other city in the world with a richer history then the Holy City where David and Solomon reigned, and where Jesus the Messiah walked, taught, was hailed as King, was crucified and resurrected. Yet it is precisely because Jerusalem is a sacred city to the world's three largest religions that the city is racked with pain, rage, and suffering.

When God creates the new heaven and the new earth, the New Jerusalem will descend out of heaven like "a bride beautifully dressed for her husband" (Revelation 21:2). Why will the New Jerusalem be so stunningly adorned? Because that city will be home to the bride of Christ, the true church of all believers. Those who love the Lord Jesus Christ, who have received Him as Savior and Lord, are the bride of Christ. We will live in the New Jerusalem. We will all be invited to the Marriage Supper of the Lamb.

The New Jerusalem comes out of heaven. God speaks from the throne, the fixed center of the universe, and He announces that

His dwelling place is now among the people. He will wipe away all their tears, and death will be no more.

If there is a burden on your heart, if there is sadness and regret, if there are tears in your eyes as you read these words, I have wonderful news for you: Jesus Himself is going to touch your eyes and wipe away your tears and take away your sorrow. There will be no hurt, no fear, no loss, no separation, and no regret in heaven. Satan will not be able to harm us or harass us there—he will be less than a memory.

A GLIMPSE OF HELL

In the midst of the vision of the New Jerusalem, the Lord speaks directly to John and gives him a message for all who read the book of Revelation: "I am the Alpha and the Omega, the Beginning and the End. To the thirsty I will give water without cost from the spring of the water of life. Those who are victorious will inherit all this, and I will be their God and they will be my children" (Revelation 21:6–7). Jesus wants everyone reading this book to have one more opportunity to receive Him as Lord and Savior.

Jesus goes on to tell John that "the cowardly, the unbelieving, the vile, the murderers, the sexually immoral, those who practice magic arts, the idolaters and all liars" will be condemned to the lake of fire, the second death (Revelation 21:8).[2] This doesn't mean that if you have committed some of these sins in the past, then you are beyond salvation. Jesus is saying that all those who continue in these sins, those who reject Jesus and refuse to repent and turn to Him for salvation have doomed themselves to eternal separation from God.

When Jesus speaks of "the cowardly, the unbelieving," He is talking about those who respond to persecution by worshipping Caesar and denying the Lord Jesus. This does not mean that a person who collapses in fear and denies Christ is beyond salvation. After all, the apostle Peter did exactly that, denying Christ three times before the crucifixion. But sinners must come to Christ and confess their sin, repent of it, and seek forgiveness.

Those who will not repent of their sin have no place in the eternal City of God. Their place, Jesus says, is in the lake of fire. If the book of Revelation teaches anything, it's that the choices we make today will determine our future. Our eternal destiny will be one place or the other. We will either be in heaven with Jesus—or in hell with Satan. There is no third alternative. Reward or judgment? We must choose.

I know how unpopular the teaching of God's judgment is today. Many ministers either avoid this subject or deny the existence of hell. There are many churches that deny the biblical doctrine of hell—the Unitarian Universalists, Christian Scientists, the assorted New Age cults, and yes, increasing numbers of Protestant churches. They preach a message that says, "It doesn't matter what you do with Jesus. God is nonjudgmental. He accepts everybody."

But if God does not judge sin and disobedience, then why did Jesus have to die?

Many times over the years I have pointed out that Jesus spoke more about hell than He spoke about heaven. And I stand by that statement.

But in recent years some people have disputed that statement.

In spite of all evidence to the contrary, they would have us believe that Jesus hardly ever mentioned eternal judgment. They say that when Jesus talked about the fires of "Gehenna" (which translates as "hell" in our English Bibles[3]), He was referring to a trash dump outside of Jerusalem, not a place of eternal punishment.

They have rationalized the story Jesus told about Lazarus, the beggar who was in paradise with Abraham while the rich man suffered in Hades. They claim that Jesus was just making a point about helping the needy. He didn't really intend for us to believe in a literal hell. Even though the Lord's teaching on hell could not be any clearer, many false teachers are twisting themselves into pretzels to avoid what God's Word plainly says.

The Bible teaches that every soul was formed in the womb to live for eternity. Every soul is immortal, but not every immortal soul will live forever in heaven. In *The Problem of Pain*, C. S. Lewis lays out the logic of hell. He explains it in the terminology of a Cambridge scholar, so to make his meaning clear, I will paraphrase his words and give you the gist of his thinking.

Lewis says, in effect, "I would give anything to be able to truthfully say, 'Everyone will be saved.' But my reason replies, 'Should God save people against their will?' The doctrine of hell is one of the main reasons non-Christians attack Christianity as 'barbarous,' and one of the main reasons they question the goodness of God. The opponents of Christianity say that belief in hell is a detestable doctrine. In fact, I detest the notion of hell myself—I hate it from the depths of my being. The problem with the doctrine of hell is not simply that God would send people to their final and eternal destruction. The problem is more difficult to understand than that:

the doctrine of hell says that God is so loving and merciful that He actually became a man and submitted Himself to death by torture to save us from eternal ruin—yet, when we refuse to accept the gift of salvation, God permits us to choose hell of our own free will, and He won't lift a finger to stop us from destroying ourselves."

That's the Youssef paraphrase of C. S. Lewis. In his original quotation, Lewis concludes: "Here is the real problem: so much mercy, yet still there is hell."[4] Lewis is absolutely right. The real question is not whether the doctrine of hell is detestable. Of course it's detestable. The notion of hell chills us to the marrow. Yet we still must answer the question, "Is it true?"

I believe that the assault on the doctrine of hell in our times is part of the satanic strategy of preparing the world for the coming of the Antichrist. Before the Antichrist (with a capital *A*) is revealed, the world will be overrun with antichrists (with a small *a*). These antichrists, these false teachers, will infiltrate the church and occupy pulpits and church leadership positions. They will write best-selling books that will be published by Christian publishers. Those books will be sold in Christian bookstores.

As the teaching of the doctrine of hell becomes increasingly unpopular, many genuine believers avoid teaching on the subject. They still believe the Bible, but they are too timid to stand up and defend biblical truth. They don't want to be attacked; they don't want to be criticized; they don't want members of their congregations getting upset and leaving the church. They won't *deny* the truth about hell—they just won't talk about it.

I once had a conversation with a preacher who said to me, "The reason I don't talk about hell is because it offends so many people in my congregation. To avoid conflict, I just avoid the subject of hell altogether and keep my messages positive."

I thought, *Don't you think I want to avoid it too?* I don't enjoy conflict. I don't enjoy being criticized. But I didn't enter the ministry to become a motivational speaker. I entered the ministry to preach the full Word of God, from cover to cover, leaving nothing out. If I "offend" a member of my congregation out of hell and into heaven, then I have fulfilled my mission.

Some people say, "The gospel is good news. How can hell be good news?" Well, the answer is obvious. It makes no sense to say we are saved unless we make it clear what we are saved *from*. We are saved *from* hell—and we are saved *to* heaven. That's the essence of the good news. Unless we speak clearly and accurately about eternal judgment, unless we make it clear what salvation is all about, we are wasting our time building churches and preaching sermons.

The Bible is clear: the wages of sin is death—eternal death (Romans 6:23). So what is eternal death? It is separation from God in hell forever and ever. That's bad news—but there is good news, the greatest news in the history of the human race. While every one of us deserves hell, God in His mercy offers us eternal life as a free gift.

You may think, *Michael Youssef is teaching Christianity 101. This is elementary.* It may be elementary to you, but there are many false teachers who are denying these simple truths—and many believers are falling for it. So I want to make sure you know that not only is heaven for real, but hell is for real as well. God is holy and just. And God is love. If you reject His love, demonstrated on the cross, then you will be judged by God's holiness—and you will receive God's judgment.

A neighbor of mine teaches a class for young professionals in a mainline denomination church. He recently told me, "We've been talking about the doctrine of hell in our class. And every person in the class agrees that God is too loving to condemn anyone to hell." Then he waited for me to respond. I'm sure he thought I was going to argue with him.

His jaw dropped when I said, "I completely agree."

He said, "Say that again?"

"I said I agree—God is too loving to condemn anyone to hell. That's why God sent Jesus to die on the cross and save us from hell. He's not willing that any should perish. But people possess the awesome, frightening power of free will. If they willfully reject the gift of salvation, they will condemn *themselves* to hell."

William Booth, the founder of the Salvation Army, is one of my heroes. He used to tell his cadets, when they came to be trained as officers in the Salvation Army, "If I had my choice, I would cancel these classes and I would send each of you to hell for just a few minutes. You would come back as great soul winners."[5]

Hell is not a metaphor or a symbol. Hell is a place. And I'm certain that everyone who ends up there will have to admit, "God is just. He did not deal unfairly with me. I got here by my own choice. I got what I deserved."

Jesus tells John that those who reject His offer of salvation will suffer "the second death." But this warning of hell is coupled with an invitation to heaven and everlasting life: "I am the Alpha and the Omega, the Beginning and the End. To the thirsty I will give water without cost from the spring of the water of life. Those who are victorious will inherit all this, and I will be their God and they will be my children" (Revelation 21:6–7).

THE EXCITEMENT OF HEAVEN

Next, an angel says to John, "Come, I will show you the bride, the wife of the Lamb" (Revelation 21:9). Then the angel takes John to a mountaintop to see the New Jerusalem. From Revelation 21:10 to 22:6, the angel takes John on a magnificent guided tour of the New Jerusalem.

The city is brilliantly lit from within by the glory of God. It gleams like a sparkling jewel, as clear as crystal. It has twelve gates, symbolizing the twelve tribes of Israel, and it has twelve foundations, representing the twelve apostles. The city is built on the foundation of apostolic teaching, and its structure consists of Old Testament prophecies.

The angel gave John the measurements of the city. It is a cube measuring 12,000 stadia in length, width, and height. Translating "stadia" into a more familiar system of measurements, we find that the city is going to be—are you ready for this?—1,400 miles long by 1,400 miles wide by 1,400 miles high. That means that each dimension of the New Jerusalem is equivalent to the distance from Atlanta to Denver, or from the Mississippi River to the Pacific Ocean.

The volume of the New Jerusalem is going to be more than 2.7 billion cubic miles. No wonder Jesus said, "In my Father's house are many mansions" (John 14:2 KJV). A beautiful, brilliant crystalline cube measuring 1,400 miles on each side contains more than enough room for a few billion mansions.

The imagery John uses is indescribably beautiful. If you let your mind's eye picture a vast crystalline structure glittering in colors of jasper, agate, sapphire, emerald, onyx, ruby, chrysolite, beryl, topaz, turquoise, jacinth, amethyst, and pure gold, you are just beginning to grasp the breathtaking beauty of the New Jerusalem. Does the new Holy City have a temple like the old Jerusalem? John writes:

> I did not see a temple in the city, because the Lord God Almighty and the Lamb are its temple. The city does not need the sun or the moon to shine on it, for the glory of God gives it light, and the Lamb is its lamp. (Revelation 21:22–23)

In the Old Testament, Moses built a tabernacle to symbolize God's presence with Israel. Later, Solomon built the first temple in all its magnificent glory—and it, too, was a symbol of God's presence with His people. The first temple was destroyed by the Babylonians in 586 BC. The second temple was built in about 516 BC. And orthodox Jews believe a third temple will someday be built on the Temple Mount.

All of these temples are symbols of God's presence, but a symbol is not the reality. When the reality comes, when God is truly and visibly present with His people, we will have no need of symbols. That's why the New Jerusalem has no temple. God

Himself, and the Lord Jesus Christ, will be present among us in the new Holy City.

There will be no streetlights in the City, nor will the City need the sun and moon. God Himself will be the Light of the New Jerusalem.

In Revelation 22, John describes the river of life "as clear as crystal, flowing from the throne of God and of the Lamb down the middle of the great street of the city" (vv. 1–2). The wellspring of this river is God Himself. The river of life flows endlessly, symbolizing the perpetual flow of blessings from the Lord.

When I was a boy, we used to sing a song written by the nineteenth-century hymn writer Robert Lowry, who wrote many beloved songs, including "He Arose" and "Nothing but the Blood of Jesus." The hymn I recall is based on this scene in Revelation 22, and the chorus of the hymn may be familiar to you:

> Yes, we'll gather at the river,
> The beautiful, the beautiful river;
> Gather with the saints at the river
> That flows by the throne of God.[6]

That river of life flows from the throne, and believers will gather around the throne and around the river. They will worship the Lord, and there will be no night in that city because Jesus Himself is the Light. And the river of life will be a fountain of continual blessing and eternal life.

The book of Revelation is intimately connected with the book of Genesis in many ways. Here we see another connection. In the

Garden of Eden, God said to Adam and Eve, "You must not eat from the tree of the knowledge of good and evil, for when you eat from it you will certainly die" (Genesis 2:17). Satan deceived Adam and Eve; they ate from the tree and discovered the knowledge of sin. In so doing, they fell from their innocent state. By disobeying God, they received the penalty of death. And the human race has been under a spiritual and physical death penalty ever since.

Our span of life on this earth is limited, and each of us has a God-appointed expiration date. I have nonbelieving friends who see me work out in the gym, and they kid me and say, "I thought you were eager to go to heaven! But here you are, trying to prolong your life by staying healthy!"

I tell them, "I'm not trying to prolong my life. We all have a God-appointed time to die. All the exercise in the world won't extend my lifespan by an extra minute beyond what God has decreed. But as long as I am in this body, serving the Lord, I want to give Him my all. And that means I need to stay as healthy as I can for as long as I can."

No one lives forever in this fallen world, but in the New Jerusalem, there will be no sickness, no curse, and no death. This will be the new Paradise, the restored Garden of Eden. Adam and Eve were expelled from the Garden of Eden to prevent them from eating from the tree of life (Genesis 3:22–24). But we will gather around the tree of life, which John says bears "twelve crops of fruit, yielding its fruit every month. And the leaves of the tree are for the healing of the nations" (Revelation 22:2). And we will enjoy the Edenic paradise that Adam and Eve lost.

John also tells us that we, God's servants, will serve Him in the new heaven. We will have important work to do—meaningful, exciting, challenging work. As servants of the Lord, we may find that our work takes us to other worlds and distant galaxies. We can't imagine all the plans God is working on in all the distant reaches of His universe. And John says that we will reign with God "for ever and ever" (Revelation 22:5).

If you have never before looked forward to heaven with eager anticipation, I hope you are beginning to catch the excitement of heaven right now. I hope you will begin each day thinking about heaven. And I hope that as you go to bed each night, your last waking thoughts will be prayers of gratitude for the wonderful gift of heaven.

Do we truly understand the destiny that is ours as God's redeemed people? If we did, we wouldn't become so easily upset by the problems we face each day. Our earthly trials are not worthy to be compared to the glorious home our Lord is preparing for us (Romans 8:18). The best way to face all of our earthly trials—including the ultimate trial, death itself—is to view all of life through the lens of our true home in heaven.

PART 5

APOCALYPSE NOW

How Revelation Impacts Our Lives Today

NINE

IF JESUS WROTE YOU A LETTER

IN CHAPTERS 2 AND 3 of the book of Revelation, Jesus dictates a series of seven letters to the apostle John, and He instructs John to send these letters to the churches in Ephesus, Smyrna, Pergamum, Thyatira, Sardis, Philadelphia, and Laodicea. Though the Lord's seven letters occur near the beginning of the book of Revelation, I chose to save these letters for last.

Throughout this study, we have been looking at Revelation theme by theme instead of chapter by chapter. I thought it would be interesting to look at the major prophetic themes of Revelation first—themes of Christ and the Antichrist, the Great Tribulation and the Battle of Armageddon, hell and heaven. Then, in light of all we have learned about God's plan for the future, the instruction in these seven letters will be all the more compelling.

I believe these seven letters become even more meaningful as we are reminded of the Tribulation, Armageddon, and the terrifying cataclysms that are coming upon the world. We realize it's not enough to simply play at church. The stakes are eternal. Whether in times of plenty and peace, or poverty and persecution, these letters tell us how to live as we await the Lord's return.

The seven letters of Jesus to the seven churches in Asia Minor are some of the most powerful, life-changing passages in all of Scripture. They penetrate our hearts, dismantle our excuses, and prepare us to live in light of the prophetic future.

The core truth of Revelation is that the Lord could return at any moment, and we need to be ready when He comes. So the central question of this chapter is, "What if Jesus wrote a letter to you, dealing with the issues you face right now, and telling you how to live faithfully until He returns?"

The answer: *He has.*

As we study these letters, we are not reading someone else's mail; *these letters are addressed to us.* So let's hear what the Lord is saying to us through these letters—and may we respond before it's too late.

By AD 96, when Revelation was probably written, there were hundreds of churches stretching from Rome and Greece, through Asia Minor, down into North Africa, and as far east as India. Why did Jesus choose to write to *these* seven churches?

Some theologians believe the seven churches represent seven ages of church history. According to this view, we are now in the seventh age, represented by the church of Laodicea, to whom Jesus said, "Because you are lukewarm—neither hot nor cold—I am about to spit you out of my mouth" (Revelation 3:16).

The Word of God is so rich in meaning that multiple interpretations of the same Scripture passage are possible. For example, these seven letters may be interpreted on one level as instructions to seven specific churches in Asia Minor, on another level as instructions to all churches in all places at all times, and on yet another level as an outline of church history. And there are probably more strands of meaning woven into these seven letters.

As you read them, you will experience a moment of recognition and think, *I know a church like that,* or, *I have a friend who fits the description,* or even, *That's me! Jesus is writing this letter directly to me.* These seven letters were written in the first century, yet they are still fresh and relevant in the twenty-first century. In every age and in every part of the world, the church of Jesus Christ needs a message of admonition, exhortation, and encouragement.

1. TO THE CHURCH IN EPHESUS

The first letter is addressed to the church in Ephesus—the church where John had been a pastor until he was exiled on Patmos. These letters are addressed to "the angel" of each church. The Greek word translated "angel" literally means "messenger," and some scholars believe Jesus addressed these letters to the "messengers" or pastors of the seven churches, who would deliver them to their congregations. Here is the message to the church in Ephesus:

"To the angel of the church in Ephesus write:
These are the words of him who holds the seven stars in his right hand and walks among the seven golden lampstands. I know your deeds, your hard work and your

perseverance. I know that you cannot tolerate wicked people, that you have tested those who claim to be apostles but are not, and have found them false. You have persevered and have endured hardships for my name, and have not grown weary.

Yet I hold this against you: You have forsaken the love you had at first. Consider how far you have fallen! Repent and do the things you did at first. If you do not repent, I will come to you and remove your lampstand from its place. But you have this in your favor: You hate the practices of the Nicolaitans, which I also hate.

Whoever has ears, let them hear what the Spirit says to the churches. To the one who is victorious, I will give the right to eat from the tree of life, which is in the paradise of God." (Revelation 2:1–7)

Ephesus was a great city in ancient times—a center of wealth and commerce with a population well over two hundred thousand. Ephesus boasted of being the site of the famed Temple of Diana, one of the Seven Wonders of the Ancient World.

The apostle Paul founded the church in Ephesus and spent more time there than with any of the other churches he founded. He spent three years teaching and establishing the Ephesian Christians. Apollos, Timothy, and Priscilla and Aquila also labored there.

John, who lived thirty years beyond the death of Paul, became an overseeing pastor of the church in Ephesus. The Ephesian church didn't meet in one church building but was divided among a number of smaller house churches that met in homes throughout the city. John was probably the overseer of this community of small, interconnected churches.

There is a lesson for us in the way Jesus deals with the Ephesian church. He found something positive to affirm before launching into confrontation. He said, "I know your deeds," and he affirmed their good deeds right up front.

This letter tells us a lot about the Ephesian Christians. They were hardworking Christians. They rejected false doctrine and believed in accurate biblical interpretation. Jesus said, "You hate the practices of the Nicolaitans, which I also hate" (Revelation 2:6). A second-century church father, Irenaeus, wrote in *Against Heresies* that the Nicolaitans were false teachers who spread the ideas of a man named Nicolas. Other churches had fallen for the heresies of the Nicolaitans, but the Ephesians had rejected them.

The Nicolaitans taught that there's no harm in sexual immorality, because fleshly sins won't affect our salvation. The Nicolaitans were like many in the church today who claim that there's no harm in sexual relations outside of marriage, that it's healthy for Christians to consume pornography like *Fifty Shades of Grey*. If you have rationalized lust and immorality in your own life, then you have swallowed the heresy of the Nicolaitans, which the Ephesians rejected.

After reading the Lord's commendations of the Ephesians, you might say, "What a wonderful, faithful, hardworking church!" Yet Jesus had one important word of rebuke for the Ephesians. I believe every Christian in the world is vulnerable to the spiritual error Jesus identifies in the Ephesian church.

Jesus said, "Yet I hold this against you: You have forsaken the love you had at first" (Revelation 2:4). The Ephesians were outwardly doing the right things—but inwardly, they had a heart problem. We easily fall into the trap of thinking that being a Christian is a matter of the right behavior. But Jesus wants us to know that the focus of the Christian walk is *our love for Him*. If we love Him, then our behavior will flow from that love. But if we lose our love for Him, then all our religious activities mean nothing.

The Ephesians were caring for widows and feeding the hungry, but they had abandoned their purest motivation for doing good works. They had lost their first love for Jesus. Outwardly, the Ephesian church was thriving, dynamic, and on the move. But inwardly, the Ephesian Christians were experiencing heart failure. They were doing the right things, but from the wrong motives.

Jesus, the Great Physician, is deeply concerned about our heart health. If your service in the church is not motivated by love for Jesus, then it's only a matter of time before you set your affections on something other than Jesus. There are five specific spiritual dangers that result from allowing our love for Jesus to fail.

First danger: *Compromise*. When our love for Jesus grows cold, we live with one foot in the world and one foot in the kingdom of God. We compromise with the world and try to maintain a lifestyle that is half Christian, half worldly.

Second danger: *Complacency*. We become complacent about sin, thinking, *Jesus has forgiven my sins. I'm eternally saved. I can live any way I choose without consequences.*

Third danger: *Coldness*. We become distant toward God. We feel entitled to God's blessings, and if He doesn't bless us in the way we want or doesn't meet our expectations, we blame God and treat Him coldly.

Fourth danger: *Complaining.* We view God as unfair. Our prayers are filled with accusations and blame: "Lord, after all I've done for You, how can You allow these trials in my life? You're so unfair!"

Fifth danger: *Craving the world.* We look at the world around we and desire the things we see. We begin to crave wealth and power and luxury.

The Great Physician has prescribed a cure for our heart failure: "Consider how far you have fallen! Repent and do the things you did at first" (Revelation 2:5). Retrace your steps. Find out where you mislaid your first love. Where did you wander from the path of your love relationship with Jesus? What seduced you away from fidelity to Him?

Jesus warned that if the Ephesians did not act quickly, He would remove their lampstand—a source of illumination. Jesus didn't say the Ephesians would lose their salvation. He was saying He would snuff out the candle flame of their witness. They would cease to shine for Christ in a darkened world.

I have been to Ephesus, and I have walked among the ruins of that city. There is no lampstand, no Christian witness, no evidence that Ephesus was once a center of vibrant Christian witness. There are many other cities across Europe and North America where thriving churches once stood. Today, they are museums. Their lampstands have been removed.

If you're just going through the motions of the Christian faith and have lost your desire for Christ, your witness for Him will go dark. Our motivation for sharing Christ with others is *love*—love for Jesus and love for others. If our love grows cold, our motivation for witnessing fails. We cease to shine for Him.

Let us love Jesus more than anything in life, more than the approval of others, more than our ideas and opinions, more than our pleasure and security, more than our plans and goals. If you have lost your first love, go to the Lord in prayer and ask Him to rekindle your love for Him. Remember all He has done for you. When He was dying on the cross, He was saying, "I love you." Don't lose your love for Him.

2. TO THE CHURCH IN SMYRNA

The Lord's second letter is addressed to the believers in Smyrna. There are many Christians going through a Smyrna experience right now. You might be going through affliction and testing right now. If so, here is the Lord's message to Smyrna—and to you:

> "To the angel of the church in Smyrna write:
>
> These are the words of him who is the First and the Last, who died and came to life again. I know your afflictions and your poverty—yet you are rich! I know about the slander of those who say they are Jews and are not, but are a synagogue of Satan. Do not be afraid of what you are about to suffer. I tell you, the devil will put some of you in prison to test you, and you will suffer persecution for ten days. Be faithful, even to the point of death, and I will give you life as your victor's crown.
>
> Whoever has ears, let them hear what the Spirit says to

the churches. The one who is victorious will not be hurt at all by the second death." (Revelation 2:8–11)

Smyrna was the home of the shrine of Caesar. In AD 26, during the reign of Tiberius Caesar, eleven cities competed for the honor of hosting the shrine of the Imperial cult. Smyrna won the honor. The Imperial cult—the worship of Caesar—reached its peak under Domitian, the emperor who exiled John to Patmos. Domitian demanded to be worshipped as *dominus et deus* ("lord and god").

In Smyrna, people went to the Imperial Shrine, burned incense before the image of the emperor, and worshipped the emperor as a god. But the faithful Christians in Smyrna refused to participate. They said, "We will only worship Jesus. He alone is our Lord and God." They risked everything to stand publicly against the Imperial cult. Christian merchants lost customers. Christian families lost friends. Many Christians were mocked, jeered, and assaulted. Some were martyred. In about AD 156, bishop Polycarp of Smyrna was burned at the stake for refusing to worship the emperor.

The Greek word *smyrna* means myrrh, a fragrant resin used for making perfume. In order for myrrh to release its fragrance, the solidified resin must be crushed. At the first Christmas, wise men from the East brought gifts of gold, frankincense, and myrrh to the baby Jesus. The gift of myrrh was significant because Jesus would one day be crushed for our sins so that the fragrance of God's forgiveness might be released.

Smyrna was named after myrrh, the city's chief export. Like

myrrh itself, the Christians of Smyrna were being crushed because of their love for Jesus. By enduring persecution for His sake, they released a sweet fragrance of the gospel. So Jesus gave them a message of encouragement, without rebuke: "I know your afflictions and your poverty—yet you are rich! . . . Do not be afraid of what you are about to suffer. . . . Be faithful, even to the point of death, and I will give you life as your victor's crown" (Revelation 2:9–10).

If you are suffering for the Lord and sacrificing for Him, then you can be comforted in knowing that He knows your afflictions. You are storing up riches in heaven, because Jesus will reward you for your endurance. The surrounding culture worships the emperor of this world, the god of this present age, Satan. But you are taking a courageous stand for Jesus in the midst of an idolatrous world. Though you are poor, you are spiritually rich.

Most Christians in America feel confident that persecution will never come here. We shake our heads when we see the horrible things that are done to Christians in other lands, but we feel safe here. I have to be candid: I believe persecution is coming to America. The warning signs are already here. If that is so, then the Lord's message to Smyrna will become very precious to us.

If you are being crushed because of your love for Jesus, then stand firm. Be faithful—and win the victor's crown.

3. TO THE CHURCH IN PERGAMUM

The Lord's third letter is addressed to the believers in Pergamum. The city of Pergamum was a cesspool of strange religious practices, from the worship of animals to the worship of idols. The Christians in Pergamum were surrounded by a culture of idolatry. Here's the Lord's message to the Christians in Pergamum:

"To the angel of the church in Pergamum write:

These are the words of him who has the sharp, double-edged sword. I know where you live—where Satan has his throne. Yet you remain true to my name. You did not renounce your faith in me, not even in the days of Antipas, my faithful witness, who was put to death in your city—where Satan lives.

Nevertheless, I have a few things against you: There are some among you who hold to the teaching of Balaam, who taught Balak to entice the Israelites to sin so that they ate food sacrificed to idols and committed sexual immorality. Likewise, you also have those who hold to the teaching of the Nicolaitans. Repent therefore! Otherwise, I will soon come to you and will fight against them with the sword of my mouth.

Whoever has ears, let them hear what the Spirit says to the churches. To the one who is victorious, I will give some of the hidden manna. I will also give that person a white stone with a new name written on it, known only to the one who receives it." (Revelation 2:12–17)

Jesus said, "I know where you live—where Satan has his throne." Jesus was not using a spiritual metaphor. He was referring to the great Altar of Zeus, the chief god of the Greek pantheon. The altar was built in the second century BC and was undoubtedly the throne of Satan that Jesus referred to. In the late 1800s, German archaeologists excavated the Acropolis of Pergamum, including the Altar of Zeus, and the altar was shipped to Germany in pieces and reassembled at the Pergamum Museum in Berlin, where it remains on display to this day.

Because these Christians lived faithfully in the shadow of this monument to false religion, Jesus commended them, "You remain true to my name. You did not renounce your faith in me, not even in the days of Antipas, my faithful witness, who was put to death in your city—where Satan lives" (Revelation 2:13).

But the church in Pergamum was not without flaws. They had permitted the false teachings of Balaam and the Nicolaitans in their midst. We find the story of Balaam in Numbers 22–24. Here's a brief summary:

Balaam was a fortune-teller, a man who engaged in the forbidden practice of divination. During the time before the Israelites entered the promised land, King Balak of Moab summoned Balaam and offered to pay him to put a curse on the Israelites.

At first, Balaam refused to speak anything except the words God gave him—words of blessing instead of cursing. In exasperation, King Balak finally said, "I brought you to curse my enemies, but you have done nothing but bless them!" Balaam replied, "Must I not speak what the LORD puts in my mouth?" (Numbers 23:11–12).

At first glance, it seems that Balaam obeyed God. But the Scriptures tell us that God was angry with Balaam for speaking to the Moabite ruler. And at one point, as Balaam rode his donkey to meet with the king, God caused the donkey to speak. Then an angel blocked Balaam's path, saying, "I have come here to oppose you because your path is a reckless one" (Numbers 22:32).

As Peter later wrote, Balaam "loved the wages of wickedness. But he was rebuked for his wrongdoing by a donkey—an animal without speech—who spoke with a human voice and restrained the prophet's madness" (2 Peter 2:15–16). Balaam had special powers from God but Balaam used those powers to enrich himself. He was an unfaithful prophet who was led astray by greed.

Later, in Numbers 25, the nation of Moab sent Moabite women to seduce the men of Israel into immorality and idolatry. God's people actually began worshipping the demon-god Baal on Mount Peor. Because of this sin, God sent a plague against Israel and twenty-four thousand people died.

Whose idea was it to send these Moabite women to seduce Israel? We don't find out until Numbers 31. There the Israelites went to war against the Midianites and killed five Midianite kings. They found Balaam among the Midianites and killed him with the sword. At that point, the Scriptures reveal that it was Balaam who came up with the idea of seducing Israel with Moabite women. The Moabites "followed Balaam's advice and enticed the Israelites to be unfaithful to the LORD in the Peor incident, so that a plague struck the LORD's people" (Numbers 31:16).

Though Balaam would not directly curse the people of Israel, he came up with an indirect approach to get God's people to *curse themselves* through sinful acts. Balaam suggested to the king of Moab that he send Moabite women to entice the Israelites with sexual temptation. Once these women had seduced the Israelite men sexually, it was easy to seduce them into idolatry.

That's a typical satanic strategy. If he can't get you to do his bidding by direct attack, then he'll work through the weakness of the flesh and maneuver you into cursing yourself. The next time you are tempted to indulge in lust, pornography, infidelity, or some other sin of the flesh, remember Balaam's plan to seduce Israel. Don't surrender to Satan.

This is the strategy Jesus refers to when He tells the believers in Pergamum, "There are some among you who hold to the teaching of Balaam, who taught Balak to entice the Israelites to sin so that they ate food sacrificed to idols and committed sexual immorality" (Revelation 2:14).

Jesus goes on to say, "Likewise, you also have those who hold to the teaching of the Nicolaitans. Repent therefore! Otherwise, I will soon come to you and will fight against them with the sword of my mouth" (Revelation 2:15–16). The believers in Pergamum were seduced by the Nicolaitans. They had fallen for the notion that immorality is spiritually harmless. They said to themselves, "We're broad-minded believers. Sexual immorality and eating meat sacrificed to idols is just part of the culture here." It is no shame to be called narrow-minded for refusing to compromise the truth of God's Word. Sometimes there is virtue in being narrow-minded. Jesus said, "But small is the gate and narrow the road that leads to life, and only a few find it" (Matthew 7:14).

Many of the Christians in Pergamum were apparently approval junkies; they wanted to be liked by their pagan neighbors. So they adopted immoral practices so they would fit in. Many Christians today are approval junkies as well—eager to compromise their Christian principles to be approved by non-Christians.

We have an obligation to love non-Christians with the love of Jesus. But we must never sacrifice God's truth in order to love them. We must never try to win them over by watering down the demands of the gospel. We should never encourage non-Christians to join the church without repentance and salvation.

Near the end of His letter, Jesus says, "To the one who is victorious, I will give some of the hidden manna. I will also give that person a white stone with a new name written on it, known only to the one who receives it" (Revelation 2:17). To understand what Jesus means about "hidden manna," look at John 6, where Jesus is questioned by Jewish leaders who seek to trap Him. Jesus says:

> Your ancestors ate the manna in the wilderness, yet they died. But here is the bread that comes down from heaven, which anyone may eat and not die. I am the living bread that came down from heaven. Whoever eats this bread will live forever. This bread is my flesh, which I will give for the life of the world. (vv. 49–51)

Jesus Himself is the manna from heaven, the Bread of Life that brings eternal life.

What does Jesus mean when He says, "I will also give that person a white stone with a new name written on it, known only to the one who receives it" (Revelation 2:17)? The Roman judicial system was not a system of trial by jury. A single judge would hear the case, render the verdict, and determine the penalty. If the defendant was found guilty, the judge would hand him a black stone. If the defendant was found innocent, the judge would hand him a white stone.

That's what Jesus says here. When we commit our lives to Him and endure opposition and persecution for His sake, He gives us a white stone. He declares us innocent. He sets us free. That is His promise to the believers in Pergamum, where Satan has his throne—and that is His promise to you and me in these dark and godless times.

4. TO THE CHURCH IN THYATIRA

The Lord's fourth letter, addressed to the believers in Thyatira, is the longest letter of the seven—and perhaps the most troubling:

> "To the angel of the church in Thyatira write:
>
> These are the words of the Son of God, whose eyes are like blazing fire and whose feet are like burnished bronze. I know your deeds, your love and faith, your service and perseverance, and that you are now doing more than you did at first.
>
> Nevertheless, I have this against you: You tolerate that woman Jezebel, who calls herself a prophet. By her teaching she misleads my servants into sexual immorality and the eating of food sacrificed to idols. I have given her time to repent of her immorality, but she is unwilling. So I will cast her on a bed of suffering, and I will make those who commit adultery with her suffer intensely, unless they repent of her ways. I will strike her children dead.

Then all the churches will know that I am he who searches hearts and minds, and I will repay each of you according to your deeds.

Now I say to the rest of you in Thyatira, to you who do not hold to her teaching and have not learned Satan's so-called deep secrets, 'I will not impose any other burden on you, except to hold on to what you have until I come.'

To the one who is victorious and does my will to the end, I will give authority over the nations—that one 'will rule them with an iron scepter and will dash them to pieces like pottery'—just as I have received authority from my Father. I will also give that one the morning star. Whoever has ears, let them hear what the Spirit says to the churches." (Revelation 2:18–29)

Jesus praises the believers in Thyatira for their love, faith, service, and patient endurance. He affirms their growth in good works, telling them, "You are now doing more than you did at first." But even though this church has many commendable traits, there's a hidden cancer of moral compromise threatening the life of the church. This cancer has a name: Jezebel.

The Lord refers to events in 1 and 2 Kings, where we encounter Queen Jezebel. She was a pagan Baal worshipper, but King Ahab of Israel foolishly married her. She turned the king's heart away from the Lord and persuaded him to set up temples to Baal. She also persecuted God's prophets. There is a lesson here: Do not be unequally yoked with an unbeliever. Do not compromise your spiritual and moral principles. Beware of the "Jezebel" who wants to seduce you away from the Lord.

The "Jezebel" in Thyatira was a false and self-appointed "prophetess." Like her Old Testament namesake, this Jezebel spread spiritual and moral compromise. Jesus said, "By her teaching she misleads my servants into sexual immorality and the eating of food sacrificed to idols" (Revelation 2:20). She claimed to speak for God, even while she was carrying out Satan's strategy of seducing believers with the temptations of the flesh.

Moral compromise and spiritual compromise always go together. When we drop our guard against sexual immorality, we open ourselves up to apostasy, heresy, and unbelief. Like a fisherman setting a hook in the mouth of a fish, Satan uses lust and immorality to set the hook in our flesh. Once immorality becomes a habit in our lives, we look for ways to rationalize our sin. And as soon we start rationalizing away biblical morality, we are halfway to abandoning the cornerstones of our faith.

One of the most foolish mantras of our times—and we hear it increasingly within the church—is, "Times have changed." What people mean is, "Truth has changed. Nobody believes in the old moral laws anymore. Nobody obeys biblical morality anymore. The old truths don't apply to the times in which we live."

But truth has not changed. In fact, every unspeakable sexual practice that is rampant in our culture today was just as prevalent in the Roman Empire. The Christian church was born into a world of incredible decadence and immorality. First-century Christians were surrounded by immorality of every description.

The "Jezebel" in Thyatira was teaching believers to give in to their sinful impulses—and she was luring them into apostasy. So Jesus said, "I have given her time to repent of her immorality, but she is unwilling. So I will cast her on a bed of suffering, and I will make those who commit adultery with her suffer intensely, unless they repent of her ways. I will strike her children dead" (Revelation 2:21–22).

Jesus wants us to know that polluting His church with sin and deception is a deadly serious matter. The spirit of Jezebel destroys churches, and that's why Jesus detests it—and why He will punish false teachers like Jezebel. He said, "Then all the churches will know that I am he who searches hearts and minds, and I will repay each of you according to your deeds" (Revelation 2:23).

That's the bad news about Thyatira. Here's the good news: "Now I say to the rest of you in Thyatira, to you who do not hold to her teaching and have not learned Satan's so-called deep secrets, 'I will not impose any other burden on you, except to hold on to what you have until I come'" (Revelation 2:24–25). The Lord has only condemnation for those who would seduce the church, but for believers who hold to the purity of His gospel, He imposes no burden.

Then Jesus makes a thrilling promise to the believers in Thyatira: "To the one who is victorious and does my will to the end, I will give authority over the nations—that one 'will rule them with an iron scepter and will dash them to pieces like pottery'—just as I have received authority from my Father" (Revelation 2:26–27). Isn't that amazing? We will reign with Him. This is the same promise Paul wrote about to Timothy: "If we endure, / we will also reign with him" (2 Timothy 2:12).

Finally, Jesus makes this promise to the faithful believers in Thyatira: "I will also give that one the morning star" (Revelation 2:28). What does Jesus mean? We find a clue near the end of Revelation: "I, Jesus, have sent my angel to give you this testimony for the churches. I am the Root and the Offspring of David, and the bright Morning Star" (Revelation 22:16).

If we remain faithful and obedient, Jesus will give us . . . *Himself.* What more could we want? What more could we ask? If we turn our backs on Satan, if we remain faithful to His truth, then we will receive eternity with the Lord Jesus as our reward.

5. TO THE CHURCH IN SARDIS

The Lord's fifth letter is addressed to the church of Sardis. This is a sobering letter. I pray that neither you nor your church is like the church at Sardis:

> "To the angel of the church in Sardis write:
>
> These are the words of him who holds the seven spirits of God and the seven stars. I know your deeds; you have a reputation of being alive, but you are dead. Wake up! Strengthen what remains and is about to die, for I have found your deeds unfinished in the sight of my God. Remember, therefore, what you have received and heard; hold it fast, and repent. But if you do not wake up, I will come like a thief, and you will not know at what time I will come to you.
>
> Yet you have a few people in Sardis who have not soiled their clothes. They will walk with me, dressed in white,

for they are worthy. The one who is victorious will, like them, be dressed in white. I will never blot out the name of that person from the book of life, but will acknowledge that name before my Father and his angels. Whoever has ears, let them hear what the Spirit says to the churches." (Revelation 3:1–6)

Jesus said, "I know your deeds; you have a reputation of being alive, but you are dead" (v. 1). Many Christians cultivate a *reputation* for godliness. They use evangelical jargon. They carry a big, black Bible. They have a fine-sounding statement of faith. But their reputation for being spiritually alive is a hollow shell. What a tragedy when the reality doesn't match the reputation.

No Christian is perfect, and neither is any church. All Christians are sinners, and all churches are made up of fallible human beings. The Lord does not expect churches to be perfect, but He does expect churches to be *alive*. If we have a reputation for being alive, yet we are dead, the Lord cannot live His life through us.

So Jesus says, "Wake up! Strengthen what remains and is about to die. . . . Remember, therefore, what you have received and heard; hold it fast, and repent" (Revelation 3:2–3). Can a dead church come to life again? Yes! In fact, Jesus gives us five steps that lead from death to life.

Step 1: *Wake up!* Open your eyes, take a good look at your spiritual condition, and become spiritually aware.

Step 2: *Strengthen what remains!* When a patient's heart stops during surgery, the surgeon doesn't say, "Oh well—lost another one." That surgeon tries to resuscitate the patient and restore life. Similarly, when the heart of a church stops beating, it needs a jolt of truth from God's Word. We need to return to the gospel and rediscover the essential truths of our faith. That's what it means to "strengthen what remains."

Step 3: *Remember what you have received and heard.* Many churches have abandoned what they have received and heard. They deny that Jesus is the only way to heaven. They deny the truth of the resurrection. They deny the authority of Scripture. The Bible says, "There is a way that appears to be right, / but in the end it leads to death" (Proverbs 14:12). To bring a dead church back to life, remember what you have received and heard.

Step 4: *Hold it fast.* Hang on to it! Guard it with your life! Protect the truth that you have received and heard. When unbelievers attack your faith from without, or Satan assails your faith from within, guard it, cling to it, and don't let go.

Step 5: *Repent.* If you are going down a path that leads to death—change course, change direction, change your mind, and change your ways.

When a church has a reputation for being alive but is practically dead, there's no time to lose. Take these five steps immediately! The Lord is patient—but His patience won't last forever. If we do not respond, if we do not wake up, Jesus says, "I will come like a thief, and you will not know at what time I will come to you" (Revelation 3:3). The words translated "come to you" would be better translated "come upon you" or "come against you." Jesus is not talking about the Rapture of the church. He is talking about disciplining the church.

There was a glimmer of life remaining in the church at Sardis. Jesus said, "You have a few people in Sardis who have not soiled their clothes. They will walk with me, dressed in white, for they are worthy" (Revelation 3:4). The church was mostly dead, but a faithful few remained.

If you are in a dead church right now, God may be calling you to speak up and say, "This church is nearly dead—but by the grace of the Lord Jesus Christ, we can inject new life into this church. We can wake up, strengthen what remains, remember what we have heard, hold it fast, and repent. Let's ask God to resurrect this church!"

6. TO THE CHURCH IN PHILADELPHIA

The Lord's sixth letter is addressed to the church in Philadelphia, and there is not a single word of condemnation in this letter:

"To the angel of the church in Philadelphia write:

These are the words of him who is holy and true, who holds the key of David. What he opens no one can shut, and what he shuts no one can open. I know your deeds. See, I have placed before you an open door that no one can shut. I know that you have little strength, yet you have kept my word and have not denied my name. I will make those who are of the synagogue of Satan, who claim to be Jews though they are not, but are liars—I will make them come and fall down at your feet and acknowledge that I have loved you. Since you have kept my command to endure patiently, I will also keep you from the hour of trial that is going to come on the whole world to test the inhabitants of the earth.

I am coming soon. Hold on to what you have, so that no one will take your crown. The one who is victorious I will make a pillar in the temple of my God. Never again will they leave it. I will write on them the name of my God and the name of the city of my God, the new Jerusalem, which is coming down out of heaven from my God; and I will also write on them my new name. Whoever has ears, let them hear what the Spirit says to the churches. (Revelation 3:7–13)

Jesus identifies Himself as the one who holds "the key of David." In other words, He is the Messiah. In the Old Testament, God promised King David a royal descendant: "I will establish the throne of his kingdom forever. I will be his father, and he will be my son" (2 Samuel 7:13–14).[1] Part of this prophecy referred to David's son Solomon (who was not yet born) and part referred to Jesus the Messiah. In many places in Scripture, Jesus is called "son of David," or a descendant of David. So the key of David speaks of His authority as Messiah.

With the key of messianic authority, Jesus says (speaking of Himself in third person), "What he opens no one can shut, and what he shuts no one can open" (Revelation 3:7). Jesus alone has the authority to open and shut the doors of history, of salvation, of heaven and hell. No other human being has the power to open and shut these doors.

One of the doors that Jesus alone has authority over is the

doorway to God the Father. He said, "I am the way and the truth and the life. No one comes to the Father except through me" (John 14:6). Now, when you tell people that Jesus is the only way to the Father, you will probably start an argument. Someone may say, "You can't say that Jesus is the only way! That's not tolerant of other religions. That's not inclusive. There are many paths to heaven."

There's no point in arguing with such people. The best response is to calmly say, "Your argument isn't with me. It's with Jesus. I didn't say Jesus is the only way. Jesus said it Himself—and I believe it. If you want to argue, then you will have to argue with Jesus."

Jesus opens doors that no one can shut, and He shuts doors no one can open. Today, Jesus invites everyone to repent and be saved—but a time is coming when He will shut the door and the judgment of humanity will begin.

Next, Jesus says, "I know your deeds. See, I have placed before you an open door that no one can shut. I know that you have little strength, yet you have kept my word and have not denied my name" (Revelation 3:8). Jesus is telling the Christians in Philadelphia that they may be weak by the world's standards, but He was placing a great opportunity for ministry before them. If they seized that opportunity, He would bless them even more.

God has blessed all of us with open doors of ministry. If God has blessed you with time, then use your time to serve Him. If He has blessed you with influence, then use your influence to serve Him. If He has blessed you with wealth, then invest it in God's kingdom. If you reject those opportunities, then He will put you on the shelf and call someone else.

The church in Philadelphia was poor and powerless, yet Jesus blessed them with an open door. Why? Because they were faithful. They did what they could with what they had. If you ever think, *I'm poor and powerless, so I have nothing to offer God,* remember that little church in Philadelphia. Remember the Lord's promise: "I have placed before you an open door that no one can shut" (Revelation 3:8).

Serve the Lord with all your might, and He will pour out His blessings on your life.

7. TO THE CHURCH IN LAODICEA

The Lord's seventh and final letter is addressed to the church in Laodicea, and it is a message of condemnation. If these seven churches represent seven ages of church history, then we are currently in the Laodicean age. And if that is so, we should weep—and tremble. The church in Laodicea is a lukewarm church, and Jesus detests lukewarmness. Tell me if this does not sound like an average respectable evangelical church in America today—a church that is neither on fire nor cold but nauseatingly lukewarm:

"To the angel of the church in Laodicea write:

These are the words of the Amen, the faithful and true witness, the ruler of God's creation. I know your deeds, that you are neither cold nor hot. I wish you were either one or the other! So, because you are lukewarm—neither hot nor cold—I am about to spit you out of my mouth. You say, 'I am rich; I have acquired wealth and do not need a thing.' But you do not realize that you are wretched, pitiful, poor, blind and naked. I counsel you to buy from me gold refined in the fire, so you can become rich; and white clothes to wear, so you can cover your shameful nakedness; and salve to put on your eyes, so you can see.

Those whom I love I rebuke and discipline. So be earnest and repent. Here I am! I stand at the door and knock. If anyone hears my voice and opens the door, I will come in and eat with that person, and they with me.

To the one who is victorious, I will give the right to sit with me on my throne, just as I was victorious and sat down with my Father on his throne. Whoever has ears, let them hear what the Spirit says to the churches." (Revelation 3:14–22)

I ask you: How can there be some sixty million evangelical believers in America,[2] yet our witness to the world remains so anemic? Why are we not seeing revival in America today? Why is immorality being normalized in the church? Why has the church embraced a culture of entertainment instead of a culture of Christian discipleship? Why are Christians more focused on success than on sacrifice? Why are believers debating such questions as "Does hell really exist?" and "Is Jesus the only way to heaven?" Why are so-called evangelicals casting doubt on essential biblical doctrine?

Is it not because the church has become lukewarm? Is it not because the American church has become the Laodicean church? As Elton Trueblood observed, "It used to be that Christianity was a revolutionary faith that turned the world upside down. But today Christians sit in Sunday morning church services looking at their watches, wondering what time dinner will be served, or thinking about the kickoff. And we hope that church won't interfere with the things we would really rather be doing."[3]

Jesus looked at the church in Laodicea and said, in effect, "I suffered and died for you. Yet you give Me one hour a week on Sunday mornings and tip Me a few dollars in the collection plate, as if I'm your waiter, not your Savior. I gave My life for you, but do you witness for Me? Do you tell your friends and neighbors about all I've done for you? Either love Me with a white-hot intensity— or stop playing church. Your lukewarmness is sickening."

Then Jesus prescribes the cure for lukewarmness: "I counsel you to buy from me gold refined in the fire, so you can become rich; and white clothes to wear, so you can cover your shameful nakedness; and salve to put on your eyes, so you can see" (Revelation 3:18).

Laodicea was a rich and prosperous city. In AD 61, Laodicea was almost completely leveled by a massive earthquake. Yet there was so much wealth there that the Laodiceans rebuilt their city very quickly—and without federal aid from Rome. The city was famed for its two principal exports: textiles and Phrygian powder, which was used as an eye salve. The Phrygian powder of Laodicea was acclaimed for its medicinal value by the second-century Greek physician Galen.[4]

Notice the Lord's irony: He tells the Laodiceans to buy three things from Him—gold so that they may become rich, clothing to cover their nakedness, and eye salve for their blindness. What was

Laodicea famous for? Its wealth, its textiles, and its eye salve. Jesus was telling them, in effect, "The very items you think you have in abundance—gold, clothing, and eye salve—are precisely the items you lack in a spiritual sense. You are poor, naked, and blind."

The Laodiceans needed a white garment to cover the shame of their sin, and that garment could only come from the righteousness of Jesus. The Laodiceans could not see their poverty and nakedness, and the salve to open their eyes could only come from Jesus. He alone is the Source of spiritual insight. "Those whom I love," He says, "I rebuke and discipline. So be earnest and repent."

Next, we encounter one of the most beloved verses in Scripture—that beautiful invitation from the heart of our Lord: "Here I am! I stand at the door and knock. If anyone hears my voice and opens the door, I will come in and eat with that person, and they with me" (Revelation 3:20).

You may be familiar with the paintings of Warner Sallman (1892–1968), such as his famed *Head of Christ* and *Christ in Gethsemane*. One of his most famous paintings is called *Christ at Heart's Door*, based on Revelation 3:20. It depicts the Lord Jesus knocking on the door, and all around the door are thorns and thistles, symbolizing our sin. And there's another detail that is easily overlooked—there is *no doorknob* on the outside. The doorknob is only on the inside. Jesus will not enter your life unless *you* open the door and invite Him in.

Jesus stands at the door of your heart and knocks. If you refuse to let Him in, He will let you have your way—and you will bear the consequences. Only you can turn the knob and open the door. If you do, He will come in and eat with you and have fellowship with you and be your Friend, both now and throughout eternity.

These seven letters of John's Apocalypse were spoken by Jesus and written to churches in the first century, yet they speak to the need of our hearts today. The book of Revelation has much to say about the future—but even more to say about the present. The Apocalypse, the revelation of God's truth, is *now*.

As we take these truths that come straight from the heart of Jesus, and we apply them to our hearts today, we will secure our eternity with Christ. As the Lord says in Revelation 3:21–22, "To the one who is victorious, I will give the right to sit with me on my throne, just as I was victorious and sat down with my Father on his throne. Whoever has ears, let them hear what the Spirit says to the churches."

TEN

COME, LORD JESUS!

DIETRICH BONHOEFFER (1906–1945) was a German pastor and cofounder of the Confessing Church, which boldly opposed Adolf Hitler's genocide and war policies. He was arrested by the Gestapo in April 1943 and spent the rest of his life in prison. The Nazis executed him on April 9, 1945.

Throughout his imprisonment, Bonhoeffer urged his fellow Christians to stand firm against Hitler. One group of believers, convinced that Hitler was the Antichrist and the end times were upon them, urged Bonhoeffer to stop speaking out against Hitler. They thought that if he would mute his criticism, the Nazis might spare his life.

"Why expose yourself to so much danger?" his friends asked. "Jesus will return any day, and your suffering will be for nothing."

"If Jesus returns tomorrow," Bonhoeffer said, "then tomorrow I'll rest from my labor. But today I have work to do. I must continue the struggle until it's finished."[1]

It's true. Jesus may return tomorrow—but in the meantime,

we have work to do. As someone once said, we must make our plans as if He will not return for a hundred years, and we must live as if He is coming today.

In the closing verses of Revelation, our Lord tells us again and again, "I am coming soon!" He wants us to watch and wait for Him. He wants us to be joyful at His appearing. He reminds us of the rewards that will be ours if we are ready when He comes:

> "Look, I am coming soon! My reward is with me, and I will give to each person according to what they have done. I am the Alpha and the Omega, the First and the Last, the Beginning and the End.
>
> "Blessed are those who wash their robes, that they may have the right to the tree of life and may go through the gates into the city." (Revelation 22:12–14)

Have you washed your robes? Are you looking forward to entering the New Jerusalem and eating from the tree of life? Do you know that your eternity in heaven is settled with Him?

If you have never asked Jesus to be your Lord and Savior, or if you are not sure whether you belong to Him, you can be certain right now. You can move from death to life before you even finish reading this book. The Lord's closing message in Revelation is a message of invitation. Jesus says:

> "I, Jesus, have sent my angel to give you this testimony for the churches. I am the Root and the Offspring of David, and the bright Morning Star."

The Spirit and the bride say, "Come!" And let the one who hears say, "Come!" Let the one who is thirsty come; and let the one who wishes take the free gift of the water of life. (Revelation 22:16–17)

Are you thirsty for life? As you make your way through this spiritually parched world, this culture of death, are you thirsty for the living God and the life He brings? Only the water of eternal life can quench our spiritual thirst. And Jesus is the only Source for living water.

Eternal life is a free gift for you and me, but it cost Jesus everything. It cost Him His agony, His blood, His life. Yet He offers eternal life to you and me as a free gift. How do we receive this free gift from the Lord Jesus? By letting Him into our lives.

Let me suggest a simple prayer of commitment—a prayer in which you simply talk to God straight from your heart. If you want this new life, if you want to commit your life to Jesus and receive Him as Lord and Savior, then pray this prayer:

Dear Lord,

Thank You for sending Your Son to die on the cross for my sins.

Be merciful to me, a sinner. I repent of my sins, and I want to live the rest of my life for You.

Jesus, I invite You to take over as my Lord and Savior. Please seal this decision and give me the strength to live each day for You.

In the name of Jesus, Amen.

If you mean business with Jesus, He will come into your life and you will become a new creation. You don't have to be afraid of the future. You don't have to fear the Great Tribulation or the Antichrist or the Battle of Armageddon. You don't have to fear death. From now on, you can look forward to the future.

Joe Stowell, president of Cornerstone University in Grand Rapids, Michigan, tells about a conversation he had with his friend Bud Wood, founder of Shepherds Home in Wisconsin, a Christian residence for people with developmental disabilities such as Down syndrome. The residents receive therapy, training, and the good news of the love of Jesus.

Once, when Joe and Bud were talking at Shepherds Home, Bud said, "Joe, do you know what our biggest maintenance problem at Shepherds is?"

"I have no idea," Joe said.

"Dirty windows."

"Dirty windows? Why is that?"

"Our kids are always pressing their hands and faces against the glass. They're always looking up at the sky to see if today might be the day that Jesus returns. They know that when He comes and takes them to His home in heaven, they will no longer have any disabilities. They'll be healed and complete."[2]

Doesn't that challenge your faith? It does mine. If we truly believe the Lord's promise that He is coming soon, shouldn't we have dirty windows? Shouldn't we press our hands and faces against our windows every day, watching for His return?

Don't you long to see Jesus? Won't it be wonderful to enter

those gates, healed and complete, with all of your infirmities and sorrows removed?

The book of Revelation closes with this thrilling promise:

He who testifies to these things says, "Yes, I am coming soon."

Amen. Come, Lord Jesus.

The grace of the Lord Jesus be with God's people. Amen. (Revelation 22:20–21)

Jesus Christ is coming for us, and it won't be long. Are you ready for His return? He could come next year. Or next week. Or in the next minute.

Are you ready?

NOTES

Introduction: The Capstone of the Bible

1. Stephen Hawking, quoted in Laurence Foss, *The End of Modern Medicine: Biomedical Science under a Microscope* (Albany: State University of New York Press, 2002), 197.

Chapter 1: The Relevant Revelation

1. Tim Arango, "ISIS Transforming into Functioning State That Uses Terror as Tool," *New York Times*, July 21, 2015, http://www.nytimes.com/2015/07/22/world/middleeast /isis-transforming-into-functioning-state-that-uses-terror-as-tool.html?_r=1.
2. Ibid.
3. Ibid.
4. Ibid.
5. John Boyd Orr, "Nobel Lecture: Science and Peace" (lecture, Norwegian Nobel Institute, Oslo, Norway, December 12, 1949), http://www.nobelprize.org/nobel_prizes/peace /laureates/1949/orr-lecture.html.
6. *Revision of the United Nations Charter: Hearings Before a Subcommittee of the Committee on Foreign Relations, United States Senate*, 81st Cong. (February 17, 1950) (statement of James P. Warburg, appearing as an individual), https://en.wikisource.org/wiki/James _Warburg_before_the_Subcommittee_on_Revision_of_the_United_Nations_Charter.
7. Lord Christopher Monckton, quoted in William F. Jasper, "The United Nations: On the Brink of Becoming a World Government," *New American*, October 11, 2012, http://www.thenewamerican.com/world-news/item/13126-the-united-nations-on-the -brink-of-becoming-a-world-government.
8. Von Michael Bauchmüller and Stefan Braun, "Bill Gates im Interview: 'Den täglichen Tod nehmen wir nicht wahr,'" *Süddeutsche Zeitung*, January 28, 2015, http://www. sueddeutsche.de/wirtschaft/bill-gates-im-interview-den-taeglichen-tod-nehmen -wir-nicht-wahr-1.2324164; translated from German with assistance from Babelfish.com and Translate.Google.com.
9. "Note on Financial Reform from the Pontifical Council for Justice and Peace," News.VA Official Vatican Network, October 24, 2011, http://www.news.va/en/news/full-text -note-on-financial-reform-from-the-pontif.
10. Cristina Corbin, "Some 100,000 Christians Killed per Year over Faith, Vatican Says," Fox News, June 2, 2013, http://www.foxnews.com/world/2013/06/02 /vatican-spokesman-claims-100000-christians-killed-annually-because-faith/.
11. "Worldwide Persecution of Christians," PrayerFoundation, accessed November 5, 2015, http://prayerfoundation.org/worldwide_persecution_of_christians.htm.
12. Editor2, "21 Egypt Christians Praised Christ before Beheadings," Religious Freedom Coalition, February 19, 2015, http://www.religiousfreedomcoalition .org/2015/02/19/21-egypt-christians-praised-christ-before-beheadings/.

13. Sylvia Westall, Ahmed Tolba, and Aaron Maasho, "Islamic State Shoots and Beheads 30 Ethiopian Christians in Libya," Religion News Service, April 19, 2015, http://www. religionnews.com/2015/04/19/islamic-state-shoots-beheads-30-ethiopianchristians -libya/.

14. William Evans, "The Book of Revelation," *The Institute Tie,* vol. 2 (October 1901): 44.

15. Ken Curtis, "Whatever Happened to the Twelve Apostles?" Christianity.com, accessed November 5, 2015, http://www.christianity.com/church/church-history/timeline/1-300 /whatever-happened-to-the-twelve-apostles-11629558.html.

16. William Barclay, *Barclay's Guide to the New Testament* (Louisville, KY: Westminster John Knox, 2008), 317–18; William Barclay, Elizabeth Mary McNamer, and Bargil Pixner, *Jesus and First-Century Christianity in Jerusalem* (Mahwah, NJ: Paulist, 2008), 77–78.

17. Ian Boxall, *Patmos in the Reception History of the Apocalypse* (New York: Oxford University Press, 2013), 110; Gordon Franz, "The King and I: Exiled to Patmos, Part 2," Associates for Biblical Research, BibleArchaeology.org, January 28, 2010, http://www .biblearchaeology.org/post/2010/01/28/The-King-and-I-Exiled-To-Patmos-Part-2.aspx.

18. *Thayer's Greek Lexicon,* s.v. "Stephanos," BlueLetterBible.org, accessed November 5, 2015, https://www.blueletterbible.org/lang/Lexicon/Lexicon.cfm?strongs =G4735&t=KJV.

19. Jill Schlesinger, "18 Scary US Debt Facts," MoneyWatch, CBS News, November 18, 2010, http://www.cbsnews.com/news/18-scary-us-debt-facts/; "Surplus or Deficit of the U.S. Government's Budget in Fiscal Years 2000 to 2020 (in trillion U.S. dollars)," Statista, The Statistics Portal, http://www.statista.com/statistics/200410/surplus-or -deficit-of-the-us-governments-budget-since-2000/.

20. James D. Agresti, "National Debt Facts," Just Facts, April 26, 2011, updated August 26, 2015, http://www.justfacts.com/nationaldebt.asp.

21. Christian Today Staff Writer, "Ousted Christian Fire Chief Files Lawsuit against City of Atlanta," Christian Today, February 19, 2015, http://www.christiantoday.com/article /ousted.christian.fire.chief.files.lawsuit.against.city.of.atlanta/48509.htm.

Chapter 2: Lord of the Beginning and the End

1. *Exploring the Middle Ages* (Singapore: Marshall Cavendish, 2006), 124.

2. See also Mark 9:2–8, Luke 9:28–36; 2 Peter 1:16–18.

3. See also 1 Corinthians 15:3–8 and Galatians 1:11–16.

4. Isaac Newton, "General Scholium," appendix to the 2nd (1713) edition of *Principia Mathematica,* trans. Andrew Motte, 1729, http://isaac-newton.org/general-scholium/.

5. Isaac Newton, *Observations upon the Prophecies of Daniel, and the Apocalypse of St. John* (1733; Project Gutenberg, 2005), http://www.gutenberg.org/files/16878/16878-h /16878-h.htm.

6. C. S. Lewis, *The World's Last Night: And Other Essays* (New York: Houghton Mifflin Harcourt, 1987), 106–7.

7. Ibid., 107.

Chapter 3: The Arrival of the Antichrist

1. Moody Bible Institute, *The Apostolic Fathers* (Chicago: Moody, 2009), 80.

3. Paul Boyer and Bernard McGinn, "Apocalypticism Explained: Christopher Columbus," *Frontline*, PBS, accessed November 7, 2015, http://www.pbs.org/wgbh/pages/frontline /shows/apocalypse/explanation/columbus.html.

4. Djelal Kadir, *Columbus and the Ends of the Earth: Europe's Prophetic Rhetoric as Conquering Ideology* (Berkeley: University of California Press, 1992), 30.

5. Muhammad Hisham Kabbani, *The Approach of Armageddon? An Islamic Perspective* (Washington, DC: Islamic Supreme Council of America, 2003), 229.

6. Samuel Shahid, *The Last Trumpet: A Comparative Study in Christian-Islamic Eschatology* (Camarillo, CA: Xulon, 2005), 114, 119–20.

7. Muhammad Ibn Izzat and Muhammad Arif, *Al Mahdi and the End of Time* (London, Dar al-Taqwa, 1997), 40–41.

8. Ibrahim Amini, *Al-Imam al-Mahdi, The Just Leader of Humanity*, trans. Abdulaziz Sachedina (Qum, Iran: Ansariyan Publications, n.d.), PDF version, http://www.al-islam .org/printpdf/book/export/html/13072.

9. Abul Hassan, "Imam Mahdi, the Universal Leader," Imam Reza Network, http://www .imamreza.net/eng/imamreza.php?id=9959.

10. AskIslamPedia, "Imaam Mahdi and the Signs That Will Precede Him," AskIslampedia .com, accessed November 7, 2015, http://www.askislampedia.com/wiki/-/wiki/English _wiki/Imaam+Mahdi+and+the+Signs+that+Will+Precede+Him/.

11. Ibn Izzat and Arif, *Al Mahdi*, 15.

12. Kabbani, *Approach of Armageddon?*, 231.

13. Ching-Ching Ni, "In Arcadia Real Estate, 4 Is a Negative Number," *Los Angeles Times*, May 21, 2011, http://articles.latimes.com/2011/may/21/local/la-me-arcadia-numbers -20110521.

Chapter 4: The Reign and Fall of the Antichrist

1. Reuters, "Prayers Inflame Tensions between Muslims and Jews over Jerusalem Holy Site: Report," *Newsweek*, June 4, 2015, http://www.newsweek.com/prayers-inflame-tensions -over-jerusalem-holy-site-report-339395.

2. Ibid.

3. Yuval Avivi, "Israeli Institute Prepares Priests for Jerusalem's Third Temple," The Temple Institute, reposted from Al-Monitor, April 9, 2014, http://www.templeinstitute.org /archive/10-04-14.htm.

4. Christopher Kemp, "University Sued after Firing Creationist Fossil Hunter," *Nature*, November 5, 2014, http://www.nature.com/news/university-sued-after-firing -creationist-fossil-hunter-1.16281.

5. CBS Los Angeles, "Lawsuit: CSUN Scientist Fired after Soft Tissue Found on Dinosaur Fossil," CBS News Los Angeles, July 24, 2014, http://losangeles.cbslocal. com/2014/07/24/scientist-alleges-csun-fired-him-for-discovery-of-soft-tissue-on -dinosaur-fossil/.

6. C. S. Lewis, *Mere Christianity* (New York: HarperOne, 2015), 51.

Chapter 5: Slouching Toward Armageddon

1. Ralph Edward Oesper, *The Human Side of Scientists* (Cincinnati: University of Cincinnati Press, 1975), 17.
2. William Butler Yeats, "The Second Coming," 1919, public domain.
3. "What We Believe: The Nicene Creed," United States Conference of Catholic Bishops, accessed November 9, 2015, http://www.usccb.org/beliefs-and-teachings/what-we -believe/.
4. Arthur William Alsager Pollock, *Colburn's United Service Magazine and Naval and Military Journal, Part II* (London: H. Hurst, 1847), 595–96.

Chapter 6: Coming Soon

1. Rhonda Howard, "He Has Conquered," The Lord's Church, April 5, 2015, http: //tlcardmore.com/index.php?option=com_preachit&id=206:he-has-conquered&view =text&Itemid=97.
2. Walter A. Elwell, ed., *Baker's Evangelical Dictionary of Biblical Theology* (Grand Rapids: Baker, 1996), s.v. "Satan," http://www.biblestudytools.com/dictionary/satan/.
3. Lee Smolin, *Time Reborn: From the Crisis in Physics to the Future of the Universe* (New York: Mariner Books, 2013), 88.
4. "After Years of Blindness, Restored Sight Brought Realization of Love," in "Four Strange Love Stories from Real Life," *Chicago Tribune,* October 28, 1900, http://archives .chicagotribune.com/1900/10/28/page/54/article/four-strange-love-stories-from-real-life.

Chapter 7: A Vision of Heaven

1. Valerie Tarico, "10 Reasons Christian Heaven Would Actually be Hell," Salon, February 1, 2015, http://www.salon.com/2015/02/01/10_reasons_christian_Heaven_could _actually_be_Hell_partner/.
2. Randy Alcorn, "Overcoming the Myths about Heaven," Eternal Perspective Ministries, April 16, 2010, http://www.epm.org/resources/2010/Apr/16/overcoming-myths -about-Heaven/.
3. C. S. Lewis, *Mere Christianity,* in *The Complete C. S. Lewis Signature Classics* (New York: HarperCollins, 2002), 112.
4. "Way beyond the blue" taken from the lyrics to "Do, Lord, Remember Me," public domain.
5. Ed Mazza, "Alex Malarkey, 'The Boy Who Came Back from Heaven,' Admits He Made It All Up," *Huffington Post,* January 15, 2015, http://www.huffingtonpost.com/2015 /01/15/alex-malarkey-boy-who-came-back-from-heaven_n_6483432.html.
6. Hank Hanegraaff, "The Boy Who Came Back from Heaven—The Story Behind the Story," Christian Research Institute, April 23, 2014, http://www.equip.org/articles /boy-came-back-Heaven/.

Chapter 8: All Things New

1. The USGS Water Science School, "The Water in You," U.S. Geological Survey, last modified July 27, 2015, http://water.usgs.gov/edu/propertyyou.html.

2. The apostle Paul makes similar statements in 1 Corinthians 6:9–10 and Galatians 5:19–21; like Jesus in Revelation 21:8 and 22:15, Paul says that those who habitually, unrepentantly commit these sins will not inherit the kingdom of God.

3. For example, in Matthew 5:29, Jesus says, "If your right eye causes you to stumble, gouge it out and throw it away. It is better for you to lose one part of your body than for your whole body to be thrown into hell." The Greek word translated "hell" is *geenna*, a transliteration of the Hebrew *gehenna*. Jesus uses this same word for "hell" in Matthew 10:28; 23:15; 23:33; Mark 9:43, 45, and 47; and Luke 12:5. The word *gehenna* originally comes from the Valley of Hinnom, a burning garbage dump that was considered a cursed place because it had once been the site of sacrifices to Canaanite gods. But it is clear that Jesus uses *gehenna* to describe a place of eternal destruction after death, where there is no hope of salvation or resurrection.

4. C. S. Lewis, *The Problem of Pain*, in *The Complete C. S. Lewis Signature Classics* (New York: HarperCollins, 2002), 621.

5. Grant R. Jeffrey, *Journey into Eternity: Search for Immortality* (Tulsa, OK: Frontier Research, 2000), 219.

6. Robert Lowry, "Shall We Gather at the River?," 1864, public domain.

Chapter 9: If Jesus Wrote You a Letter

1. See also Matthew 21:15; Romans 1:3; and Revelation 22:16.

2. David Masci, "Compared with Other Christian Groups, Evangelicals' Dropoff is Less Steep," Pew Research Center FactTank, May 15, 2015, http://www.pewresearch.org /fact-tank/2015/05/15/compared-with-other-christian-groups-evangelicals-dropoff-is -less-steep/.

3. Melvin Newland, "Elton Trueblood Wrote, 'It Used to Be That . . . ,'" SermonCentral .com, February 2001, http://www.sermoncentral.com/illustrations/sermon-illustration -melvin-newland-quotes-bookofrevelation-evangelismhowto-churchpurposeof-1549.asp.

4. William Mitchell Ramsay, *The Letters to the Seven Churches of Asia and Their Place in the Plan of the Apocalypse* (London: Hodder and Stoughton, 1906), 419.

Chapter 10: Come, Lord Jesus!

1. Roy B. Zuck, *The Speaker's Quote Book: Over 5,000 Illustrations and Quotations for All Occasions* (Grand Rapids, MI: Kregel, 2009), 453.

2. Adapted from Joseph Stowell, "Dirty Windows," *Strength for the Journey*, entry for December 23, 2015, http://getmorestrength.org/daily/dirty-windows/.

ABOUT THE AUTHOR

MICHAEL YOUSSEF, Ph.D., is the founder and president of Leading The Way with Dr. Michael Youssef, a worldwide ministry that leads the way for people living in spiritual darkness to discover the light of Christ through the creative use of media and on-the-ground ministry teams. His weekly television programs and daily radio programs are broadcast more than 4,300 times per week in 24 languages to more than 190 countries. He is also the founding pastor of The Church of The Apostles in Atlanta, Georgia.

IF YOU ENJOYED THIS BOOK, WILL YOU CONSIDER SHARING THE MESSAGE WITH OTHERS?

Mention the book in a blog post or through Facebook, Twitter, Pinterest, or upload a picture through Instagram.

Recommend this book to those in your small group, book club, workplace, and classes.

Head over to facebook.com/worthypublishing, "LIKE" the page, and post a comment as to what you enjoyed the most.

Tweet "I recommend reading #EndTimesSecret by @MichaelAYoussef// @worthypub"

Pick up a copy for someone you know who would be challenged and encouraged by this message.

Write a book review online.

WORTHY®
PUBLISHING

Visit us at worthypublishing.com

twitter.com/worthypub

worthypub.tumblr.com

facebook.com/worthypublishing

pinterest.com/worthypub

instagram.com/worthypub

youtube.com/worthypublishing